AGING
Artfully

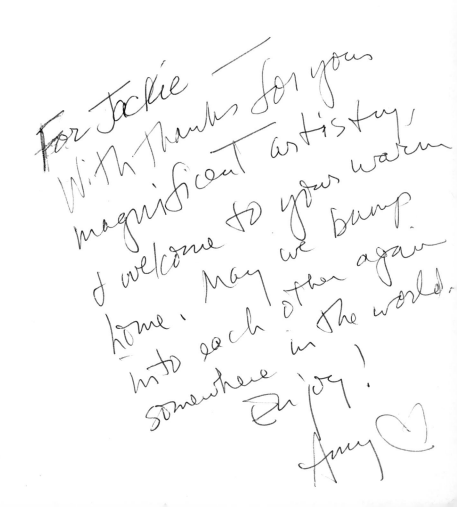

For Jackie —
With thanks for your
magnificent artistry,
& welcome to your warm
home. May we bump
into each other again
somewhere in the world.
Enjoy!
Amy ♥

AGING

Artfully

12 PROFILES:
VISUAL & PERFORMING
WOMEN ARTISTS
AGED 85-105

AMY GORMAN

and

"7 Songs of Women's Lives," a CD by Frances Kandl
A musical tribute to the women in *Aging Artfully*

PAL PUBLISHING
BERKELEY, CA

Copyright ©2006 by Amy Gorman
PAL Publishing
1563 Solano Ave., #455
Berkeley, CA 94707
palpublishing@gmail.com
www.goldenbearcasting.com

Design: Kathy Lee. Litho Process, Alameda, CA
Typefaces: Adobe Caslon for body, Univers bold condensed, Zapfino, Trajan
Printed in the USA

Publisher's Cataloging-in-Publication
Gorman, Amy.
Aging artfully : 12 profiles : visual & performing women artists aged 85-105
Amy Gorman. – 1st ed.
p. cm.
Includes compact disc.
With: 7 songs of women : a CD / by Frances Kandl. The compact disc,
7 songs of women, contains songs about the lives of seven specific women profiled in Aging artfully.

LCCN 2006905450
ISBN-13: 978-0-9785192-0-9
ISBN-10: 0-9785192-0-5

1. Older artists – California – San Francisco Bay Area – Biography.
2. Women artists – California – San Francisco Bay Area – Biography.
3. Aging. 4. Self-actualization (Psychology) in old age.
5. Women – Health and hygiene.
6. San Francisco Bay Area (Calif.) – Biography.   I. Kandl, Frances. 7 songs of women.
II. Title. III. Title: Visual & performing women artists aged 85-105.
IV. Title: Visual and performing women artists aged 85-105.

N8356.A43G67 2006   704'.0846'09227946
                QBI06-600261

Second Printing

Photos – front cover: Lily Hearst, 105, pianist, photo: Ira Nowinski
Mary Beth Washington aka Orunamamu, 85, storyteller, photo: Amy Gorman
Frances Catlett, 97, painter: background art

Photos – back cover: from left to right - Dorothy Takahashi Toy, tap dancer; Frances Catlett, painter; Faith Petric, folk singer; Grace Gildersleeve, rug braider; Isabel Ferguson, aka Betty Peterson, actor, painter, illustrator, assemblage artist; Stella Toogood Cope, storyteller; Madeline Mason, doll maker, sculptor; Elsie Ogata, ikebana artist; Rosa Maria Morales Escobar, singer, folklorico dancer; Ann Davlin, aka Grace Lowell, dancer

DEDICATION

To the memories of my parents
Minna Schrank Wiltchik   1903–1976
Philip Wiltchik   1907–1978
and
my maternal grandmother Fannie Bisgeier Schrank   1888–1956
For your devoted love

and

In memory of Stella Toogood Cope and Lily Hearst

ACKNOWLEDGMENTS

I have many people to thank.

First and most important, I thank the 12 women who with open hearts shared their personal lives with me. The trust and generosity of spirit shown me proved invaluable in the process of writing their stories. I am indebted to all the family members of those interviewed for continued interest and cooperation.

For suggesting wonderful women for this project some of whom were interviewed, others not, I thank Hal Aigner, Sherlyn Chew, Donna Davis, Mijo Horwitz, Maria Micossi-James, Betty Kano, David Lei, Lili Lim, Raquel Lopez, Rina Margolin, Mari Perez, Janet Petroni, Naomi Puro, Eleanor Walden, Empress Yee.

For reading early versions of the profiles and offering encouragement and conversation, I thank Maureen Farr, Jessica Heriot, Annette Hess, Joan Krasner Leighton, Susan Parker, Jacqueline Rouse, Diana Shye, Lois Silverstein, Annita Clark Weaver.

For adding an unusual touch of beauty and warmth to the project, I thank the musicians of the Crones' Kwartet: Debra Golata, Cathy Allen and Rachel Durling, who lent their valuable time, with Frances Kandl, to rehearse and perform the songs on the CD.

For inestimable help along the way, I thank the following people: Connie Andersen, Susan Barnert, Ernest Bicknell, Debbie Brennan, Joe Brennan, Vangie Elkins Buell, Patty Caouette, Ming Chi Carroll, George Cohen, Kathy Connelly, Pauline Cutress, Rose Dodds, Margret Elson, Estelle Freedman, Judith-Kate Friedman, Audrey Goodfriend, Margarita Hernandez, Stu Kandell, Sara Katz, Renya Larson, Carol Levy, Brian Lipson, Susan Lundgren, Mary Lyons, Kate Marks, Paul Matzner, Maria Mayoral, Oakland Museum of California (Marcia Eymann, Barbara Henry), Jorge Santis, Margot Smith, Sherry Streeter, Marion Thompson, Sharon Thompson, Judith Turiel, Stephanie Weber, Warren Wechsler, Paul Weisser, Mark Wong, Avis Worthington, Greg Young.

For ingenious ways with design, I am indebted to Kathy Lee, and I thank her for working beyond the call of duty.

For editorial and writing assistance I extend special thanks to Paulette Burnard, Arnie Passman, and Anne Rowe.

For her unflagging patience and enthusiasm I thank Patricia R. Elmore, without whose editorial help I would still be bogged down in the Introduction.

My husband, George C. Gorman, is a constant ray of sunshine in my life. He provides a daily dose of humor for which I am ever grateful. During this project he gave me the greatest gift of support, which was staying out of my way.

My adult sons, Ari and Phil, are always there for me in the cheering section. I thank them most of all for teaching me about love.

I extend deep gratitude to those mentioned above, and to those I may have omitted inadvertently.

CONTENTS*

*The ages stated are the ages of the women in 2006, except for Lily Hearst and Stella Toogood Cope, who predeceased publication of this book.

ON CREATIVITY

Down in front of my apartment building I stood waiting for a friend… Near me, barely visible in the tall grass, a pipe started spewing soap suds. I could smell laundry detergent…Two little girls came by. They squatted down to look. I heard them saying something like, "Magic! Magic bubbles! Fairy foam? Yes! Coming up from way, way down deep in the earth when there's a magic…" At that point a Grown Up came hurrying along. She paused just long enough to look down at the children and say in a loud voice, "That's overflow from some washing machine up in the apartment building." She hurried on. The little girls immediately scrambled to their feet and ran away. How I wish the Grown Up had kept quiet. Magic! Washing machines! The children had been building a fairy tale – imagining, creating.

Isabel Ferguson, age 89, April, 2006

"Every child is an artist. The problem is how to remain an artist once one grows up."

Pablo Picasso

Dorothy Toy and Amy Gorman   *Photo: Diana Shye*

INTRODUCTION

"Woke up one morning, age was on my mind."

Amy Gorman

I held Lily Hearst's 107-year old hands four days before she died, just three years after we met. My memory of her is a blessing I carry with me as I move through my own seventh decade.

Lily was the first of the remarkably vital women in the San Francisco Bay Area – all between 85 and 105 – whom I met and interviewed for this book. My friend and colleague, Frances Kandl, a composer and pianist, knew Lily. Curious about aging and wanting to explore it in all its dimensions, especially the artistic, I had asked Frances to introduce me to Lily and join me in a conversation with her.

At 105, Lily was the oldest person in Berkeley, California. She was a pianist who practiced scales and played pieces every day. Creativity was at the core of her very active daily existence.

In no time, Frances and I embarked on *Project Arts and Longevity*: I to interview the women and chronicle their life stories, Frances to write songs about them. We presented three performances of the songs, and the women were thrilled to have their lives honored and recorded. Frances performed on piano along with three musicians on cello, violin and voice.

Later, videographer Greg Young, who had already produced a film about Orunamamu, the free-spirited storyteller included in this volume, joined the project. Greg began filming the other women artists with whom we were conversing. His stirring documentary, *Still Kicking*, follows six of the women.

Aging Artfully is the culmination of this collaboration. Each of the twelve chapters profiles one of the interviewees, and is illustrated with photographs from her life. The CD of songs composed by Frances, "7 Songs of Women's Lives," is inserted in the back of most books.

All the dozen women interviewed for this book were living independently, and were still practicing artists at the time of the interviews. You may not find much about them through a Google search, but each of them, to varying degrees, has achieved at least a modicum of recognition for her chosen artistic endeavor.

I chose the 85 year mark as a starting point for many reasons. First, we have too long ignored the fact that the over-85 age segment is the fastest growing of our population. Second, half of all baby boomers will live at least to the age of 85.[1] And sadly, almost half of all people over 85 have some degree of dementia.[2] Our society is facing a demographic revolution – are we ready?

Until now, few studies have focused on the impact of creative activities on the over-85 age population, but there is reason to believe that creative engagement significantly contributes to what we might call "successful aging." The largest study ever conducted on aging in the United States – entitled *Successful Aging* and published by researchers John Rowe and Robert Kahn in 1999 – found that *involvement in social and recreational activities [including the arts] is one of three key factors in "successful aging"* (author's italics).

Gene Cohen, M.D., Ph.D., Director of the Center on Aging, Health and Humanities at George Washington University spoke at the White House Conference on Aging in December, 2005 as the nation's leaders in aging convened to shape government policy for the next decade. His long-term research on creativity and the elderly indicates that seniors who participate in arts activities enjoy better overall health, visit doctors less frequently and use less medicine, to name a few of the benefits.

The impact of the research could have a profound impact not only on the quality of life for the very old, but on the economic well-being of the country. For example, we might see huge decreases in Medicare/Medicaid spending. [3]

In writing this book, I encountered many surprises. Some of the questions I asked the women did not interest them at all – they could not pinpoint their artistic regrets, how they might have done things differently, or advice they would give younger artists struggling with the creative process. What did interest them was conversation, so sorely absent in their worlds where many friends and family have died or live far away.

Many of the women discovered their art late in life; others were dancing or singing almost from the cradle. For all of them, art is the central force that keeps them going, sustaining them in the ninth decade and beyond. Their art is now so deeply ingrained in their beings that they cannot separate it from themselves. The art and the person have merged.

None of them complained; they have no time or inclination to ruminate or dwell on negative thoughts. They accept their limitations and get through the tough times with a resilience they have learned over a lifetime. All the women eagerly welcomed the opportunity to share their lives, especially to talk about their art, and they continue to do their art no matter what.

As independent thinkers they form a Hallelujah Chorus, if you will, saying, "No thank you, but I'd like to stay at home as long as I am able." All are healthy women, having dodged chronic illness. Each follows a regular schedule of activities, looks forward to every moment. Indeed, they live in the here and now.

Our talks nourished me. I returned home from the interviews exhilarated, fueled with the desire to preserve their stories. It became clear that each of us, if we follow our passions, can live vibrantly in our old age, should we be lucky enough to get there.

I hope these women inspire you, as they have me, to develop a new vision for growing old. This is an urgent social need that mirrors the civil rights and women's movements, insisting on respect and inclusion. It is a vision of the world, as Laura Carstensen writes in *Stanford Today*, "… in which the last stage of life could be the most emotionally meaningful stage of life." She sees it as a time "… when people have the perspective that only the passage of time can afford to access life fully, to appreciate that bad times pass and good times are precious, to reap the benefits of relationships that have spanned a lifetime and to build lives that fully reward every day."

Aging Artfully is written from the women's own words, from their perspectives. It is conversational and personal. For this approach, I am indebted to Barbara Meyerhoff's *Number Our Days*, a seminal oral history of Jewish American women.

Meyerhoff, an anthropologist, recognized that her subjects' highly individual reminiscences were historically significant. So while my primary focus is on the lives and the art of my subjects in and of themselves, I trust that this book may also capture the historical memory of the last century.

Join me in a celebration of long, rich lives.

Amy Gorman,
May, 2006

[1] Thomas Perls and Margery Hunter Silver, *Living to 100*, Basic Books, 1999

[2] Ken Dychtwald, *Age Power*, Putnam Books, 2000

[3] National Center for Creative Aging, e-newsletter, "Creativity Matters," February, 2006

Lily Hearst, 105   *Photo: Ira Nowinski*

*"I practice scales and chords every day so I don't forget
them. They are precious to me. Everything goes but the
piano — the piano doesn't go away. That is forever."*

Sonata in Three Centuries
LILY HEARST
PIANIST

May 31, 1897 – January 19, 2005

*"One is born with a talent… Then you develop it… You practice every day…
But you cannot make it if it is not inside you."*

Prelude: About four weeks before Lily's death at age 107, I am sitting in the North Berkeley Senior Center listening to her warm up with Bach's *Invention #8*, and then I hear her play Chopin's *Fantasie Impromptu* and Mozart's *Turkish March*. Her arm strength is amazing. The Mozart requires big muscles for its octave passages, and Lily applies her great determination to hit *most* of the notes.

On January 19, 2005 Lily died of natural causes in her sleep in her own home. She had suffered from fatigue for about three weeks prior to her gentle passing. I feel honored to have known her and to have been there to say my farewells within days of her death.

Lily's life spanned three centuries. I first interviewed her on her 105th birthday, May 31, 2002, then several more times over the next two-plus years. Based on our many conversations, this is what I wrote about Lily in 2004.

Lily never drank coffee. But she does adore a small glass of cherry heering, "a shlup," before she goes to bed. She never smoked. She practices on her cherished Schiedmayer grand piano daily, from 8-9 a.m., always beginning with scales and chords. Lily has definite ideas about piano

Kurt, Lily, Grete (Margaret), 1900

practicing, and believes she must practice daily or she will not have a good day. She plays at the North Berkeley Senior Center just before the noon lunch, as she has every weekday for thirty years. "I practice scales and chords every day so I don't forget them. They are precious to me. Everything goes but the piano – the piano doesn't go away. That is forever," she says.

She proudly wears neither hearing aid nor glasses. She now walks with a cane, but at a pace hard to keep up with. About five feet, a striking petite figure of a woman, Lily's fine sculptured bones carry not a spare ounce of flesh. She is spectacular as she lifts her leg effortlessly, like a dancer, when I remark on her limber moves.

Her small bony frame gives no indication of the robust, muscular woman of her early family photos. She was an ardent mountaineer and skier for years. And only when about to turn 105 did Lily give up her daily swim at the Berkeley City Club, a venerable Julia Morgan-designed building. She cited her growing fatigue, a feeling that she was sinking, and the coldness of the water.

Lily is piercing in her attentiveness, and she expresses herself with the presence and precision of someone half her age, clearly and with a keen intelligence. Her memory seems remarkably intact. She is stunning in her command of language, English being her third.

Lily ID, 1908

Her speech reflects the cultured refinement of her Viennese heritage; her voice is strong and emphatic, heavy with an Austrian accent. Lily's manner, confident yet insistently modest, gives her an air of old world graciousness and European aristocracy, tempered by the liberal politics of a Jewish immigrant.

Hirsch family, 1938

She laughs easily and jokes often. After playing the piano for a while, she says smiling, "Have I played *enough* for you, yet?" But she moves me to tears with stories of her friends and relatives during the Nazi era in Austria in the 1930s. She conveys deep gratitude that she and her family were spared, and she cannot thank the American people enough, especially the Quakers who helped re-settle her. "I never forget that we were so lucky to come here – and the others perished."

She was born Lily Roger in Oswiciem, Austria, what is now Auschwitz, Poland, the third child of a middle class Jewish family. The family moved to Vienna when Lily was a young girl. "My mother was a darling… I *never* was so good." Her father, a state employee, was a disciplinarian. Lily became an obedient child, never causing trouble. "Mistakes over there [in Europe] are punishable because everything should be perfect! One learns as a child to obey. No one resisted. It's much better here [in America]."

Her sister Margaret, five years older, later became the first woman pharmacist in Vienna. The two remained close friends throughout their lifetimes. Her brother Kurt, two years Lily's senior, "was the creative one, the real rebel. Being artistic he had a rebellious nature, and my mother let him do anything he wanted." He became a composer, left for England and eventually married Joy, an Irish woman, who remains one of Lily's dearest friends. Kurt never achieved fame during his lifetime, but his music has been played frequently in Europe, posthumously.

Lily was baptized in a Methodist church as a child, a common custom among assimilated, intellectual Viennese Jews at the time, perhaps to avoid anti-Semitism. Her freethinking family didn't believe in religious precepts or in perpetuating Judaism. Lily still believes that today, and she welcomes the intermarriage of Jews with non-Jews.

There being no kindergarten, she started school at age six. Her favorite memory of school was the singing, because it was "so good to develop your personality." She also began her piano studies at six. "It was the trend. Everyone took piano lessons." At the lyceum (high school), she learned French and English in addition to all the other academic subjects.

In summers, the family frequented the Viennese region's lakes and rivers where Lily soon learned to swim. After watching her siblings swim, she thought she could too. One day they just threw her in the water. "You jump into the Danube; the rush in the river holds you down under water. If you don't fight it, the river takes you back up. It was dangerous but we all survived."[1] Later, she would swim across the Danube just for the challenge of it. Today, she feels swimming is the only sport for an older person. She says passionately, "Never give it up! I tell people keep it up… don't give up!"

During her youth, Lily heard all the great virtuosi in the grand concert halls of Vienna. This began her lifelong love of opera, especially Mozart and Wagner. Remembering Pablo Casals in concert, she says, "Unforgettable! He closed his eyes when he played… the whole concert. I went to all his concerts… naturally, everybody in Vienna went."

During her adolescent years she and her sister learned to ski and climb mountains. "Everyone in our circle did. We looked down on the ones who

*Lily as
sportswoman*

With Shareshian grandchildren, John and Steven, 1965

didn't!" They were peoples' sports, which means you didn't need much money to do them.

The sisters, Lily claims, were the first women to ski in Austria. Women skied in Sweden and Norway, but not Austria. They even challenged the prevailing fashions. She and Margaret were the first European women skiers to wear pants instead of skirts. As the trend-setting, independent spirits they were, she says, they would "not ski in skirts like the Norwegians," and their pants garnered extensive newspaper publicity at the time. Skiing was a beloved sport all her life until, at age 88, a car hit her, breaking both her legs. She recovered fully, but her skiing days were over.

About mountaineering she rhapsodizes, "To be alone in that mountain… you are in another world, in heaven." She smiles radiantly; her joy is palpable.

Lily climbed mountains during every vacation. All through her twenties she went alone with a guide. "That's how you did it, or with another girl and a guide. You were with that guide for a week, and they didn't touch you. It wasn't like now when you'd be afraid to go and be alone with them."

She learned to rock climb, using a rope and wearing shoes made of a linen-like material; there was also canoeing, horseback riding, tennis. "Life can be wonderful," reflects Lily, "when you have your health… many people are afraid. They stay in. I didn't stay in. I think that's how I got so old."

Although her sister and brother went to the University after high school, Lily did not. Her family had limited means, and being of a practical mind she decided to start earning money by working in a bank. She continued to play piano, but "I didn't want to strive to play professionally because there was too much competition. I wasn't good enough. I thought I'd be starving all my life."

In fact she was close to starving during World War I. "I remember well when I was hungry… It hurts a lot when you're hungry." She says, "It wasn't easy to endure. Finally we got some food when the peasants from the country came and sold some of their things in the city."

Her twenties were marred by one problem only – she wasn't yet married and, at thirty, she feared she might never meet the right person. Her mountains meant more to her than any man she knew. She says, "I fell in love with the mountains more than with men."

Finally, she met "the man," Alphonse Hirsch, a German Jew. They met on a ski train. John Hearst (Lily's son) says, "Alphonse was a skilled mountaineer and skier, and it was this connection which initially brought them together. Climbing mountains was one of their great joys."

"He had climbed Mont Blanc!" exclaims Lily. It meant the world to her that he was a strong mountaineer. She adds with a smile, "He liked me very much because I was a better skier than he." Remembering the Sports Train that took them on long trips through the mountains, she muses, "What better way is there to know who a man really is than to see him when he's hungry, he's cold, and he has to sleep on hay? Many marriages were performed on account of the Sports Train."[2] But for Lily and Alphonse the road to matrimony was not so simple. She could make a commitment, but could Alphonse?

Freud was all the rage in Vienna at the time, and analysis was *de rigeur* among Lily's circle of educated friends. Freud's student Wilhelm Reich was a fellow skier, and Lily underwent three years of analysis with one of his colleagues. Alphonse worked with Reich himself, and during the course of the psychoanalysis was persuaded to commit to marriage. Lily doubts he would have otherwise.

They married in 1929, and the marriage was a

Hearsts at Golden Gate Park Aquarium, 1969

good one. The Hirsches (they changed their name after World War II to Hearst) were happy in Vienna. They had two children, Helga, born in 1931, then John, four years later. Lily never took to housewifely duties easily; she found cooking and cleaning difficult but it was her nature to buckle down and "do the job well."

By then the Nazis had taken over Germany. Lily was sitting in the Opera House in 1938 when Hitler invaded Vienna. As she and friends left the Opera House people were already being rounded up by the Gestapo. They were lucky to be ushered out to safe transport home.

"Art should be separated from life. If the work he wrote was great, I go for the work and not the person."

Alphonse's job as the bank record keeper made him indispensable to the Nazis, so while thousands around them were arrested, Lily's family was spared. But knowing they could not remain safe in Austria for long, the family fled to England by train. Miraculously, they managed to get all their belongings out of Vienna including Lily's prized Schiedmayer piano, which is in her home today.

Leaving Vienna and adjusting to her new life in the U.S. was the most difficult time for Lily. In addition to the horrible turmoil going on in the world and inside herself, she remembers, "I was very unhappy when I didn't have a piano. It was something of me – like a person."

Her family eventually settled in New Jersey where Lily brought up her two children in the "American way." They joined Scouts and attended public school. They met few Europeans. Lily, although she often felt lonely, busied herself adjusting to the new culture while her husband commuted to New York City.

Language was a minor problem. She laughs, recalling her struggle with vowels. Opening her mouth wide, Lily emits a variety of choking sounds to demonstrate how hard the short /a/ in "apple" was for her. Neighbors were friendly and helped her at blending into the culture. To express gratitude to

Lily teaching exercise in Berkeley public school, 1978

the community that had taken them in, she gave free piano lessons, mostly to the young scout members.

She moved to Berkeley in 1970 to be near her son, a professor at the University of California. Alphonse died in 1978. Finding herself widowed at 81, Lily poured her energy into her longtime passions. She joined the Berkeley Hiking Club, she swam, met fellow skiers on the slopes near Lake Tahoe, and taught piano. She pursued all her favorite activities with fire – Lily has never done anything halfway.

Postlude: Until she died, Lily lived in a cottage behind her son's house, where she taught piano to a few select senior students – only those over 70.

Lily at 105 and her student, Robert A. Harris

Marjorie Jackson, her best friend and a former oboist with the San Francisco Symphony, was one of them. Robert A. Harris was thrilled when she made an exception and accepted him in 1999 at the tender age 63. He called her a fierce, demanding teacher. "Lily was merciless when I played too loud for her taste."[3] Though he attempted to control his volume, "even at the last lesson Lily complained that my trills were too loud, and they often were too slow for her taste." He'd have to play them over and over before she'd finally say, "You've got it!"

"Bach must sing," she loved to say. She was also clear that "there is no vivace in Bach." She insisted the tempo be strict and that phrasing in Bach was crucial. She'd tell Harris to "take a breather" to indicate the silence between phrases. Every section of her revered *Well-Tempered Clavier* that he played was her favorite, "the best of all!" With regard to the contrapuntal nature of Bach's music Harris often asked her if she could hear all the voices with their proper weights. "She always told me that she could hear them all. That was important to me," Harris adds.

Wagner was another of Lily's favorite composers. In our dialogue about whether art can be separated from the artist, Lily commented, "He was a terrible man. But art *should* be separated from life. If the work he wrote was great, I go for the work and not the person. I'm the loser if I don't."

Lily was a woman of strong opinions voiced articulately and often in a genteel manner. "The modern world is too fast, young people today are too noisy, so ill-behaved. When I was young I knew how to behave in public…" But she was far too polite to say that to most people. If you were to tell her, "I think the young people of Berkeley are basically well-intentioned, just brought up differently," her answer might be, "You are probably right, my dear. I'm just not used to it."

Her politics were liberal, and though she could be critical of American government, her gratitude to her adopted country would never allow her to denounce it. But for all her loyalty to the country that saved her life, it was obvious that a large portion of her vibrant heart still beat for her beloved Vienna and its surrounding lakes and mountains. Her eyes shone unmistakably brightest when she spoke about her early life in Vienna and her ecstatic experiences in the mountains of Europe.

Lily made a long, slow adjustment to the homogenization of American life. She opened her heart to people of all backgrounds, though at times she could not help but voice her annoyance at the ignorance or coarseness of people around her. Then a little snobbishness, even a tinge of bigotry, could reveal itself. But it was not her nature to dwell on this, and she continued her daily treks to the Senior Center – a melting pot of every Berkeley

Lily with friend Marjorie Jackson in "How Berkeley Can You Be" parade, 105 years old

Hearst family, Lily's 100th birthday, 1997. From left to right: Leslie Hearst, Jean Hearst, David Hearst, John Hearst, Helga Shareshian, Lily Hearst

type, from working class to leisure class, from the mentally acute to the downright mentally unbalanced. Lily's tolerance was often tested, but her graciousness and good breeding won out.

Her life was ordered until the end. Lily ate dinner with her son and his wife, sometimes saw the grandchildren and great grandchildren, and often was included in her family's extensive social life. She said, "My life is concentrated now. I don't go out very much… and I don't need entertainment. I like quiet when I'm home… and that's the blessing of getting old."

I am picturing her today arriving at the Senior Center, as on so many other days for the past thirty years, sitting down at the piano in the spacious community room, and making Bach sing.

[1] "The Reflecting Pool," Jane Gottesman, *Women's Sports and Fitness Magazine*, Sept. 1995

[2] ibid

[3] Robert A. Harris, Draft, *Lily as Piano Teacher*

Lily, 107, "How Berkeley Can You Be" parade

Gizella and Lily, 1982

REMEMBRANCES OF TEA AND THE MELTING POT

by Frances Kandl, Composer

LILY AND MY MOM, Gizella Czeizler-Kandl, 1892-1984

Lily sits with my mother on the sofa, sharing tea and cookies, at my mother's small Berkeley apartment sometime in 1982. They talk about the Berkeley Senior Center, the situation in the Middle East, where to buy the freshest vegetables and, as always, life in the old country. At 85 Lily is five years younger than my mother.

Though they are both from pre-World War I Europe, both Jewish and both participants in an Austro-Hungarian heritage, in many ways they couldn't be more different. While both are less than five feet tall, Lily is lean with angular, refined features and has an intense staccato delivery; my mother is plump, rosy-cheeked with soft features, has a relaxed demeanor and a melodious voice. Lily comes from a cosmopolitan city, and my mother from a small farm village.

Their personalities reflect the social and economic context of their early years. Though both ended up in America, married to successful professionals, their cultural differences reveal themselves in very different musical and literary tastes, as well as in their sense of fashion. My mother's love for opera extends as far as Puccini, Verdi and Franz Lehar, whereas Lily appreciates everything from early Baroque opera to Mozart and Richard Strauss. Lily loves chamber music, Schubert lieder, Bach partitas, Beethoven sonatas. My mother may swoon over a Chopin polonaise but finds anything by Bach repetitive and boring.

While Lily plays the great works of Chopin, Bach and Mozart, my mother sings Hungarian gypsy songs in a high lyrical soprano and vigorously dances the csárdás at any opportunity. Lily would have enjoyed hearing my mother sing Hungarian songs, accompanied by my father on violin and me on piano, just as my mother could have delighted in hearing Lily play Chopin's *Fantasy Impromptu*. But, in fact, music is something they never share. Their thing is tea and talk.

Lily reads the *Wall Street Journal*, my mother reads the *Readers Digest*. Both have read the world's great novels and poetry. Lily's literary tastes were formed by the best lyceum of Vienna; my mother, self-educated in two worlds, developed a cultural hodgepodge. Like Lily, my mother can enjoy *Anna Karenina* and the poetry of Schiller, but she also resonates to popular novels and poems reprinted in *Dear Abby*. Lily watches *McNeil-Lehrer* and informative programs on PBS. My mother watches mainstream news and every rerun of "The Sound of Music."

Lily always dresses impeccably (a la Neiman-Marcus) in well-designed starched blouses with tasteful ties and scarves. My mother is happy to be comfortable in synthetic stretch pants and T-shirts or sweatshirts (a la J.C. Penny). In hot weather, she is not above donning a garish muumuu!

Their divergent tastes, however, seem not to matter. They see in each other what they want to see: vibrant, warm-hearted, loquacious European women who share gratitude towards the country that rescued them, and a hatred for all tyranny and oppression. They both love good Viennese pastry and hate the Republican Party.

It is a tribute to Lily that she sees only the best in my mother and can admire her character without ever looking down on her educational shortcomings. It is a tribute to my mother that she is not intimidated by Lily's fine education and relates to her simply and directly, woman to woman. In Europe they would probably never have had occasion to speak to one another, much less drink tea together. Throughout both their lives, adjustment to American democratic society has not been easy. Both have had to deal with a more egalitarian world whose ideology, if not always its practice, is tolerance and equality. This has produced not only a financial leveling, but an attitudinal leveling as well. They now belong to the same vast American middle class and enjoy the same standard of living.

Though from different European social classes, either one is capable of displaying a hint of intolerance when confronted by ethnic differences, and yet for the most part they have both managed to overcome these biases and make friends with people who would never have crossed their paths in the "old country."

My mother once said to me that until she came to America she doesn't remember ever seeing a colored person. She means no harm with that phrase, but I had to remind her that it is now considered derogatory and might offend her faithful companion, Dorothy. She protested, saying, "Dorothy doesn't mind at all, she told me so." But Dorothy loves my mother and cuts her a lot of slack, knowing she is an old dog from the old country, and not about to learn any new tricks. Similarly, Lily is forgiven some outdated old-world attitudes and loved for her vivaciousness, her obvious sociability, her outspoken manner.

Long after my mother was gone, and Lily then well into her second century, she spoke of Gizella with more tenderness than I would have expected from their brief friendship. "She was such a wonderful woman, so lovely, so full of grace. I will never forget her." It was clear she meant it. The bond between them predates their late-in-life acquaintance.

Frances Catlett at 92

Photo: Jonathan Eubanks

*"I face an empty canvas, then begin; the brush moves, and
I watch the miracle happen."*

The Elegant Canvas
FRANCES DUNHAM CATLETT

PAINTER

Born July 3, 1908

"It takes a lot of energy to create.
If you're using energy elsewhere, you don't create."

Frances, a highly acclaimed professional visual artist, is exhibited widely in such established venues as the Oakland Museum, Yerba Buena Gardens in San Francisco and the Berkeley Art Center. There are some sixty collectors of her work according to the catalogues she meticulously maintains. Her paintings range from somber to light both in theme and color. Working in large brush and palette knife strokes, she paints landscapes and people, using realistic, abstract and introspective approaches.

She thinks in grand, bold concepts. She says, "Art is an expression with the use of paints that somehow cannot be put into writing. It covers all that we know about the universe, all that we do not. I am in awe of the universe. It looks like it's going to be here forever, but I have no answers. Art allows us to express the complexities we cannot write about."

I was introduced to Frances through one of the videos produced by the African American Library in Oakland, established to archive the lives of prominent Bay Area black citizens. At that time, in 2003, the Women's Cancer Resource Center was exhibiting some forty of her works, and I went to see them (Frances is a colon cancer survivor of fifteen years). Her canvases were rich with color, abstract design and intriguing subjects like voodoo, mysticism, and the birth of the sun.

Frances is the youngest

I couldn't wait to meet her. Though reluctant to share her life stories, many of them painful, Frances finally agreed to talk with me at Strawberry Creek Lodge, an independent living facility in Berkeley where she lives in a one-bedroom apartment.

At 96, Frances, an African American with skin nearly wrinkle free, walks with back straight, gracefully, and with a purposeful gait. Her tall, lean body, often clothed in warm-up sweats, is as energetic as her mind. With the weekly Scrabble game, twice-weekly bowling plus her many other interests, it's hard to find time for interviews. There are the family papers she is working on, letters to write legislators on behalf of progressive causes, and long walks. Frances credits her longevity to lifelong physical activity. And, as a dedicated baseball fan, she rarely misses a Giants game on TV.

She tells me she was mugged recently. As she got out of her car at the bowling alley, two guys knocked her down and snatched her purse with 50 dollars inside. After recovering from the shock, she thought how much worse it could have been and went on with her day. Frances never misses a beat.

She attributes her inner strength to her parents. Born on the same plantation in Virginia in 1862 and 1863, her mother was African American and her father, John Taylor, was the son of a Native American black woman and a white auctioneer. Many years later John's father called him to "receive the legacy." But when he arrived in Virginia, "John Taylor refused it because his father was still doing to his cousins what he had done to his mother."

Her parents moved to Hartford, Connecticut where they raised

Frances in tree, age 10

nine daughters and a son in a predominantly white neighborhood. Frances, the youngest, was born when her mother was in her late forties. Her father was a "hard shell" Baptist minister, a pastor without a pulpit, but a pillar of the church. Their church, the Union Baptist Church, was finally built in 1889. Later they bought another building which is listed in the National Historic Registry.

Their family motto was "make it do; do without; mend it; fix it." Her mother was a farmer at heart and quickly became an urban gardener. She filled their shelves with home-canned fruits and vegetables from her garden, and rarely served anything she didn't grow. Fortunately, on Saturdays, Reverend Taylor brought home pounds of beefsteak, lamb and ham. "Mary," he'd tell her mother, "the children have to eat!" Frances laughs with glee, remembering this and the festive times when her father made ice cream and root beer for them.

Her childhood, Frances says, was a happy one, partly because she and her nine siblings were so close. They had assigned chores every day – like laundry on Mondays and ironing on Tuesdays. One of her jobs was to separate the burnt-out coals from the usable ones in the cinder pile. Frances learned discipline and cooperation from watching the older ones; they had fun, but obeyed their parents and were high achievers. It was what was expected.

Two of her sisters were artists so it never occurred to Frances that she could be one, too. At ten she wanted to be a dancer, but dancing was a sin. Instead, she concentrated on her schoolwork and, perched in an apple tree

Frances, about 45

Frances, center, at faculty wife dance

behind the house, spent hours reading everything she was allowed. Of course, the books approved by her parents made no mention of sex, a topic never discussed in her religious family. The only love that mattered was God's love for your soul.

Frances tied as valedictorian in her high school class where she was one of only four black students (one of two in elementary school). Later she wondered if the other girl won because she was white. She remembers being called "nigger" as she walked home from school, and her older sisters chasing after the taunters. Frances always told herself, "Sticks and stones may break my bones, but names will never hurt me." But years later, after studying African American history, Frances knew she was an "unconscious victim of racism." The remarkable and heartbreaking story of her people in this country instilled both confidence and anger in her, and she admits she still has anti-white feelings.

Her high school achievement did not go unnoticed. A philanthropic black family in her community gave her a full scholarship, which she used at the University of Chicago so she could stay with a sister who lived in that city. There she married Albert Dunham, a philosophy graduate student and brother of the Afro-Cuban dancer Katherine Dunham. They went to Massachusetts where he had a fellowship at Harvard, and she finished her B.A. at Boston University. She was blissfully happy.

As a faculty wife and a post-graduate student at Howard University in Washington, D.C., she enjoyed a rich cultural and intellectual life. Howard was "a great mecca at that time." Frances says, "I lived in rarified air –

I would open my palms and gifts fell in them." She danced, sang, worked and, in 1933, had a son, Kaye.

Not long after that, Frances' happy life took a somber turn. Albert suddenly became ill, too ill for Frances to care for him. He was confined to an institution never to recover. Frances divorced him in 1940, and he died in 1949. The tragedy left her irreparably melancholic. She began writing poetry, which for many years got her through her despair. In a poem entitled *Mated*, she writes:

> "When, all aware, you went away
> In jealous grasp of Death, a lover,
> My bruised heart was left to start its dying."

Her other solace was music, and she regularly attended the National Symphony in Washington.

In 1942 Frances married John Catlett, the brother of sculptor and graphic artist Elizabeth Catlett. Their son Michael was born in 1944. Two years later John Catlett fell ill and died, and at age 38 with two young sons, Frances was a widow. A year later, encouraged to start a new life in California, she moved to San Francisco. "Once you have gone through a serious depression, you know you can always manage," she comments.

Frances and the two boys lived in San Francisco with the Reverend Howard Thurman and his wife Sue for about a year while Frances got on her feet. Reverend Thurman, formerly Dean of Religion at Howard University, had been recruited to help found the Church of the Fellowship of all People in San Francisco. Frances loved being part of this warm, religiously diverse community.

Frances at 25

Hiking Desolation Valley Wilderness, Lake Tahoe, late 1960s

In 1947 she received an M.A. from Mills College in Oakland, where she was probably their first black student. In 1948 she was among the first black social workers hired by the San Francisco Welfare Department. She explored various areas of government social work, with particular interest in aid to indigents, foster care, and adoptions. In 1963 she received her MSW from UC Berkeley. From 1964-68 she was assistant professor at the Graduate School of Social Work at Sacramento State, then joined the staff of Hidden Villa, a Quaker-based youth camp dedicated to bringing black and Native American children into "white" summer camps. Her swan song as a social worker was a major set of guidelines she created for infant group day care named PINC, Parent-Infant Neighborhood Center.

"Art is an expression with the use of paints that somehow cannot be put into writing."

By then Frances had taken a free art class at the de Young Museum in San Francisco. Her confidence was buoyed by a teacher who framed one of her paintings and said, "Look what you did!" Encouraged, she took more classes at the San Francisco Institute of Fine Art and the UC Extension Art Department. Eventually, she studied under Richard Bowman, a specialist in color. "He was so wonderful," she reminisces. "He taught me to see color in all its many dimensions." She was off on a new trajectory, as an artist.

Frances doesn't plan her work or think about what to paint. "I do not make sketches for a painting," she says of her creative process. "To me, that puts limits on the work. Most often, I face an empty canvas, then begin; the brush moves, and I watch the miracle happen." She never reworks a painting. "I trust that when I put something on the canvas there's a reason for it. The picture emerges. I don't know why I do it the way I do. Evidently I put on colors that mix with what's on there."

At the height of her painting she discovered four themes: "I realized the abstracts are the universe – all that we do not know about; the dancers are because that's what I wanted to be; the landscapes are from my love of nature's beauty and from my time spent hiking and camping; the people are because I enjoy being with them."

In 1978 she married Matt Crawford, a political activist known as "Mr. Berkeley." She hiked with him and they often traveled abroad together. She remembers their house on Delaware Street quite fondly.

Today she has a small studio in the activities area at Strawberry Creek Lodge where she paints when she can. Her small bedroom is filled with finished canvases waiting to be designated to family members. But her paintings aren't the only legacy for her family.

As the last of her generation, Frances feels responsible for transmitting the rich story of her family – the professors, musicians, writers, artists, educators, and the baseball player restricted to the Negro League before Jackie Robinson shattered baseball's color barrier. Frances is working on the Family Tree, currently over 50 pages; she wants each member of the family to have his or her history with photos.

"My mind wants to do some of the things I used to do, but my body doesn't let me," she says. The reality is that Frances' energy would boggle the minds of people half her age. Days she doesn't bowl she takes

Bowling, 1995

Frances at 94 with her paintings

forty-minute walks, making sure some of it is uphill, enjoying the lovely gardens of her neighborhood. And twice a week she drives to join her team for bowling –"my low-life pleasure," she calls it. She laughs comparing her art and bowling interests. "I go from the sublime to the ridiculous."

Frances isn't a church-goer these days, though she devours books on a multitude of spiritual practices. Her sacred time is Monday afternoons, when she plays Scrabble with four other women. They are severe around their game, never uttering a word until the timer beeps, except to challenge each other. "We have a great group here. We play for five hours straight without stopping."

About her residence she says, "You make acquaintances somehow. The people here have no idea of any of the things I've been through, though some of them know I paint. Your friends and family – that's different. They know you." Family, for example, call her Frank, not Frances. She adds,

"My life has been very full really… I guess everybody's life is full of *something*."

Frances dreamt of having yet another exhibit, preferably a retrospective. Her dream came close to being realized in May 2005 when the Joyce Gordon Gallery on 14th St. in Oakland exhibited much of her work. Rising to the occasion, Frances gathered paintings from her family's homes, and had a magnificent opening reception.

Now there are the stacks of papers on the living room table to deal with. And since Strawberry Creek only serves dinner, there is breakfast and lunch to prepare. Frances buys the healthiest ingredients she can find for her meals and chuckles that her son is always bringing sacks of vitamins.

She comments, "I'm really lazy. I still feel guilty when I'm having fun doing the things I love to do, like bowling, watching Jeopardy, Tiger Woods and sports TV."

Frances' energetic spirit is perfectly caught in this excerpt of a poem she wrote many years ago, *Restlessness*:

> This spring, and I swear it, I acted my age
> Until a willow a-greening caught my gaze.
> My voice tore upward
> Burst the sky door.
> Celestial pottery was jarred to the floor.
> A lyre string snapped;
> The gods worried their hair!
> And the Why was I, daft from scented air.

Postscript: *May 17, 2006 was the last day of the 2005–06 bowling season for Frances' Women's League. Frances bowled a 200, the highest score for the League, and put her team in first place.*

Ann as vampire, age 23, 1933

"*There's a source of creativity in all the children and if you step aside it will come out. Then you can guide their creativity. You do it from the inside out.*"

Jung and Dancing from the Inside Out
ANN DAVLIN aka GRACE LOWELL
DANCER

Born May 24, 1910

🦋

"You don't just hear, you hear from the depths. It has to come from here (touching her heart). If your body goes into it, then it's yours."

Ann, her stage name and the one I know her by, describes her creative process as a dancer and teacher of dance. She has enjoyed long, successful careers as both.

Now, at 93, her bulk fills the wheelchair. Her blue eyes sparkle under the shock of short, white hair, and she takes time to gather her thoughts before speaking. "The best thing I could do is to relate people to their depths and talents, and bring them forth to the outer world."

Ann says that after meeting dancers or students, she went home and moved as they moved, walked as they walked. Once she knew how it felt being in their bodies, she understood their challenges and could guide her students through them. Using this technique she teaches me, I imagine being in that chair having so much body. I want her to be my teacher.

Her house, a venerable Berkeley brown-shingled home not far from the University, is warm and inviting, with red fleur de lis wallpaper covering the large two front rooms. The heavy burgundy velvet curtains that separate them, now somewhat frayed and tatty, must have been once resplendent. Ann chose them to transform her living room into a theatrical space. Now they harbor the pungent aroma that bespeaks medicine, sickness, old age.

Ann

Born Grace Lowell in 1910, Ann grew up in Richmond, California, a town or two north of Berkeley. Her father's family boasted illustrious literary figures, as well as university presidents and business people.

James Russell Lowell, the writer, was her great-uncle, and she is also related to the poets Amy Lowell and Robert Lowell.

Her mother's people came West in a covered wagon, and from that side of her family Ann learned Virginia reels, other folk dances and songs galore. "I was fortunate to be brought up surrounded by music." Indeed, music danced into her soul.

Ann held center stage in the family until, around her fifth birthday, her sister Diana was born. The girls had a grand time together, especially singing and dancing for the family. In time, they were joined by their youngest sister Mary. Their mother encouraged them, putting her favorite records on the old Victrola, songs by Galli-Curci and other Caruso-like opera stars.

Every Saturday afternoon the sisters went to the local theater. They paid the dime admission, bought a nickel candy bar, and settled in the front row of the balcony to watch the "short subjects," such as a Disney cartoon, the newsreel, and the feature film, maybe an "Our Gang" or "Keystone Kops" comedy. Then came the big moment – the vaudeville show!

"How I loved those dancers, singers and acrobats! It thrilled me to watch the house lights dim and a colored spotlight follow the principal around the stage. In imagination I was that entertainer in the spotlight… the center of attraction… wearing theatrical makeup and frizzy hair and a costume that sparkled all over and sent reflections of light to every corner of the theater." [1]

Ann's family could not afford dance lessons for all three daughters so Ann, the oldest, who held great promise and enthusiasm, got the lessons. She taught her mother and sisters everything she learned. "Alas," Ann says, "Richmond was the boondocks, where the only classes were in tap and the national dances." Undaunted, she and Diana worked out their own routines, incorporating increasingly complex steps. Then, donning glittery costumes they performed locally, with little sister Mary making it a trio for a while.

Their "pro" opportunity came around 1930 when Al Silva, proprietor of the Silver Dollar Café in El Cerrito, discovered Ann and Diana at a performance at the Shriner's Lodge in San Francisco. Ann was then a student at U.C. Berkeley and Diana was still in high school. Silva advertised the duo as the D'arcy Sisters, and Grace Lowell became Andrea D'arcy, or Ann for short.

The girls performed first at fund-raisers, supper clubs, then nearby night clubs including El Cerrito's Kona Club, the It Club and the In and Out Bar, Oakland's Gay Nineties and Chinese Gardens, and San Francisco's Venetian Villa and the Lion's Den ("Don't worry about us, Mom," they kept reassuring her). Next, they set off on state-wide tours learning the ways of the club and bistro world ("the life"). In those Depression days, they were thrilled to be earning money.

Soon came billings with the Rockettes at Radio City Music Hall and the Ballet Moderne, and travels with the Orpheum Circuit. During World War II, they entertained soldiers stationed on the West Coast. Those were boom times for dancer-singers, a job was always to be had, as sister Diana (England) wrote in her book about their career, *Born to Dance*, with a foreword by Ann.[1]

In her twenties, Ann

Ann holding baby brother, father behind with cat, mother sideways behind Diana

Ann and Diana, 1920, at 10 and 6

continued working toward an academic degree, taking classes in child psychology at UC Berkeley, with a focus on the development of children's natural abilities. She earned her teaching credential from San Francisco State University and her Master's from Mills College.

But her real passion was dance. And she wanted to be more than a song-and-dance performer. She longed to learn ballet at a technical level not taught locally, so she enrolled in classes at the Royal Ballet of London. It was there, during the many summers of study with the masters, that she had her first real dance training and began incorporating the movements of her body into her soul. Adoring it all, working eighteen-hour days, from the nightclub circuit she moved into the world of classical ballet.

Jungian psychology was another major influence. "I wanted to get it from the horse, always wanted to go to the horse. So I went to Zurich where Karl Jung was working. I wanted to work with someone on my personal relationships."

So while studying ballet in London during the summers, she went to Switzerland to work with Jung's disciple, Dr. Guggenbuhl-Craig. Her work with him empowered her to dance more freely, and greatly influenced her later teaching. Using Jung's approach of bringing out not only the bright side of the self, but the dark, "shadow" side as well, she helped her students discover their "deepest parts" and release their creativity.

"I believe the creative process is finding where you are psychologically wounded, healing those wounds, then developing your art through discipline," she says.

In a paper, *Jung's Contribution to the Art of Dance,* Ann wrote,

"What comes from the unconscious has purpose... Martha Graham and Jung's ideas come together. She was endeavoring to get to the roots of her being, to find and express her inner myth, to reawaken and make clearly visible the savage and beautiful inner landscape where the action occurs. Jung was working with methods that will enable us to discover our center and hear the inner cry. He strove to bring illumination to the part of us that guides our destiny and causes the action."

In Europe, Ann also learned the Stanislavsky method, which teaches actors to be their characters: "When you run like a mouse, how do you run?"

Ann on right and Diana, 1929

"...if I can keep discovering things in my old age I think you go on forever... and I am dis-covering new things all the time..."

For the rest of her career, Ann combined the Stanislavsky method, Jungian psychology and her Royal Ballet training to develop her own style and technical abilities. She passed these skills on to her students.

During World War II Ann married Haskell Charles Davlin. The war had ended and he was en route home to her when he was caught in crossfire and killed. Ann kept Davlin as her last name and never remarried.

Back in California after World War II, "I would take my acrobatic mat and go teach dance in different towns. I believe dancing inspires the soul. It requires discipline and love... and an understanding of beauty." She began teaching kindergarten to earn money for basic necessities, while continuing to study dance and theater in Europe during summers.

Ann loved teaching young children and brought dance and creativity a la Jung into her elementary school classes. "There's a source of creativity in all the children and if you step aside it will come out. Then you can guide their creativity. You do it from the inside out." She taught in Lafayette and other public schools until she retired at 65.

Around 1950 she brought to fruition a dream she held for many years: that of starting a dance school. She built a studio behind her Berkeley home and enlisted sister Diana to help. At The Ann Davlin School of Dance they taught tap and ballet based on the syllabus of the Royal Academy, which still sends delegates every year to see her students perform and credential the teachers.

"Ballet is for everyone with the discipline to dance. It is not for the select few with long legs and short,

Ann left, and Diana, 1934

Ann and Henrietta, both students of SF State

square torsos."

At her school, Ann taught her students how to free their creativity, then discipline it into art. "It's like I try to take what nature gave them and build on it, keep them in touch with their basic self." As for technique, she strove to teach "how the body can move in its most exquisitely, beautiful way. Ballet goes toe to toe," she adds, "but how does the eyelash move?"

For many years, Ann was the expressive arts teacher at the Guild of Psychological Studies, based in Four Springs, California. Combining music and dance with Jungian and theatrical training, she helped students access and release their fears. For example, she'd ask them to move around in a brown cloak to protect them from the hostile forces they were dealing with. "From my way of thinking, it is not healthy for the development of the soul and the psyche to break them up into this and this and this, this is music, this is dance. They're all just one big *balloo!*" No wonder Ann was an adored teacher.

One of her former students, Alicia Lundgren, now at the Alvin Ailey School in New York, recalls, "She was strict, even yelled but her standards were so high I didn't mind. She even let us do what we wanted at the end of a lesson, usually with a scarf." Just a few years ago Ann, past 90, retired from teaching dance, passing the mantel on to Mary Lyons.

When she was about 80, dissatisfied with the drugs her physician prescribed, Ann found a psychologist through the Over 60 Clinic (now Lifelong Medical Care). The psychologist, Laura Carstensen, became one of Ann's favorite people

Ann as Gypsy Dancer about 1933

Ann, second from right receiving certificate from the Royal Academy of Dance, 1965. From left to right: Rosemary Saylor, Diana England, unknown, Ann, Geannde Herst

Ann, right, at Guild for Psychological Studies Christmas party, about 1985

– and the feeling was mutual. "She has such a discerning mind, like you couldn't put anything over on her." Her work with Carstensen led to Ann's inclusion in the Stanford University researcher's articles on aging and an appearance as a featured "old" artist on The Today Show.

Though these days Ann moves very slowly and uses a walker, her mind is crystal clear. She keeps up a busy schedule which includes teaching five piano students. She relishes conversation – about the state of the world, or the influence of religion on art – weighty topics! But she especially enjoys talking dance and her teaching techniques.

"I felt I was doing more than just teaching an art and how to point your toe; I was also helping with the souls of people." And, she adds, "Religion is the greatest art. The artistic and religious concepts are close, but the arts don't exactly spread war so much." Her favorite composer is Messaien, "so mystical," and she idolizes Margot Fonteyn. "She never lost her spontaneity. And she could do triple turns, stand on one toe for five minutes – she could do all that wonderful technical stuff."

Ann smiles as she articulates her current thinking. "People want me to be what they think their version of me is. That is not how I am… if I can keep discovering things in my old age I think you go on forever… and I am discovering new things all the time, and old things come back in a different guise."

Ann hopes to convey to younger teachers her method of combining spontaneity and disciplined technique. "A talented interpreting artist is what we're trying to develop," she says.

Ann wants you to learn to live in the moment, from the heart, for then you honor your life as art and feel whole.

[1] Diana England with foreword by Ann Davlin, *Born to Dance: The D'arcy Sisters Discover There's No Business Like Show Business.*

Postscript: *Since August, 2005, Ann has been living in a skilled nursing facility in Santa Rosa, California. During a visit with her in April, 2006, she extolled the talents of the chef, calling one of the celebratory dinners, "like a night out on the town." Her spirits are indomitable; her adjustment to this life change is inspirational.*

Ann at 93   Photo: Paula Eidson

Orunamamu at 82   *Photo: Paula Eidson*

"I need to spread the word about stories. When you have a story, tell it to someone!"

Yellowlegs, The Storyteller
MARY BETH WASHINGTON
aka ORUNAMAMU
STORYTELLER
Born April 4, 1921

"All artists had a difficult time early on."

Always on the move, Orunamamu stays alert for any opportunity to tell a story. Putting on her stethoscope she announces, "I'm a practicing storyteller instead of a practicing physician. You have to listen, anyway."

With a colorful jester's hat and a shepherd's crook, wearing layers of long, loose clothing in varied patterns, Orunamamu is an unexpected vision coming down the streets of Rockridge, a chichi neighborhood in Oakland, California where she lives. Her dancing eyes and dazzling smile tell you of the fire within. She greets you with a big "Hello there" or a hug, and proceeds to tell a story. No matter whether you are receptive or not, her tale grabs you so you have to hear it to the end.

Later, as we sit on the purple front steps of her house (her true home, she says, though she seldom sleeps there), she stops a young man pushing a baby stroller to squeal over her newest neighbor. She and the father laugh together, and anyone who passes by can't help but join in.

"My grandmother used to say, 'Hush your mouth, child. Don't you know it's your time to listen and my time to talk? When you're older, people will be listening to you.'"

So young Mary Beth listened as Grandma told stories while quilting with other older women of their community. Her grandma was prescient.

Orunamamu in street clothes

Sure enough, now she as Orunamamu, tells stories that illuminate the magic in everyday life. "What if our books were burned?" she ponders loudly. "All we would have to go on is what's in our heads."

Mary Beth is constantly outspoken and speaks frequently to strangers. She engages them in matters of importance by questioning their values, right there, on the spot. At Berkeley High School where a young math teacher has allowed her a short interlude for storytelling, I tag along. Facing the laid-back students, some snickering, she looks straight at them. "Telling stories," she begins earnestly, "is about speaking up. We all belong to the same big family and have the same smell." That gets their attention.

Later, we go to lunch and I hear her story. Ever a free spirit, Orunamamu has had four husbands, the first two black, and the next two white men. I'm not surprised to hear that she's a longtime pacifist, but what is surprising is that she grew up in a military family. Born in Huntsville, Alabama in 1921, one of nine children, she was raised in various southern military towns. We see our first sign of the unconventional Mary Beth when she says she used to hide her father's shoes so he couldn't report to duty at 5:00 a.m.

To escape washing dishes and other chores, she hid in the chinaberry tree with a book. She read her favorite stories over and over, adoring the words. Her other passion was radio. In the days before television, she affirms, your imagination supplied the pictures for the words.

Her father, a staff sergeant in charge of supplies, ran the family with Swiss clock precision but was also very generous. He handed out leftover food to the neighborhood kids to keep them healthy and save their families badly needed money. He taught her the keys to success: "energy, honesty, ambition," and, she adds, "the opportunity. You always have to find the opportunity for all those good qualities to work."

Her mother's priority was their education. Dressed in her best – silk stockings, high heels and gloves – she went to the chaplain to plead for "a military school for our Negro children." He was sympathetic but could do nothing. So she went to the sergeant, who said he could do nothing either, then to the lieutenant, the major and the colonel. Always the same story: "Sorry, my hands are tied." Finally she went to the general. "If you want a teacher," he said, "you find her and house her."

And that's what they did. They hired Ms. Lee, an African American teacher, to start the first Negro school in Fort Benning, Georgia. When asked what she learned from her mother, her face brightens. "Stickability," she says.

> ## "We all belong to the same big family and have the same smell."

Mary Beth got her degree in English and home economics at Paine College, a Georgia school with an interracial faculty. Shortly afterwards, in 1943, her family moved to Milwaukee, Wisconsin where her favorite aunt lived.

Despite her college degree, Mary Beth's first jobs were at a candy factory and boatyard. Returning to school, she received a master's in education and psychology, then taught elementary school in Milwaukee for several years. Meantime she married and had two sons. But after eight years with her increasingly abusive husband, she knew she had to get away. Only, where could she go that he wouldn't find her? At that time there were no shelters for battered women.

Then a lady at the African American Methodist Church she attended with her mother and aunt brought Mary Beth a newspaper clipping. It told of a wealthy woman in Pasadena, California whose husband had accidentally backed the car over two of their children. Surely, thought

Mary Beth, a woman who had lost two children would understand the plight of another mother fleeing an abusive husband. And he'd never find them in California.

Mary Beth had only learned to drive six weeks before but she didn't hesitate. She put her sons in the car and headed across country. Driving through Utah she noted a sign: "Teachers Wanted." Well, it wouldn't hurt to apply, so she did a quick clothes change, interviewed for the position and then drove on to California.

Shortly afterward, a woman in Pasadena opened the door to find a stranger and two little boys on her doorsteps. Mary Beth was right about the woman. She took them in and gave them a home while Mary Beth looked for a job.

She had accepted a teaching position in Pasadena and had long forgotten her interview in Utah when the Bureau of Indian Affairs sent her an offer to teach the Navaho. The idea of expanding her horizons and exposing her sons to a different culture appealed to her, so she convinced the Pasadena school administration that the experience would make her a stronger teacher when she returned to teach there the next year. Then she set off to work with the Navaho.

Since the only churches available in Utah were Mormon, Mary Beth tried to join one but was turned away because at that time African Americans were barred from Mormon churches. She found a Quaker group which readily accepted her and her sons, so she metaphorically thumbed her nose at the Mormons and began her lifelong affiliation with the tolerant, welcoming Quakers.

She met her second husband, Tousant Jennings, when she returned to Los Angeles. He was a wonderful father to her sons, but not interested in sex, so they finally divorced. In 1959 she moved to Berkeley where she met Jack Smock, the love of her life.

An engineer, he taught her how to whittle as they listened to the music at the New Orleans Jazz Club in the Claremont Hotel. They had a lot in common, for Jack was a rebel too – in his case, against an overbearing father. "I regained my self-respect with him and we had great times together," she says. "The problem was his father was a racist, and when I visited I had to stay in a motel."

She bought her house in 1969 with her own money because Jack, rejecting his father's capitalist values, didn't believe in owning property. Then, after ten happy years of marriage, Jack left her for another woman.

It was a terrible blow. Not one to brood too long, she was soon back at the Claremont's jazz club, this time dancing with Don Stofle in 1972. It was only after their wedding the next year that she realized he was an alcoholic, but she stuck with him for the next twenty years, until his death.

It was Don who gave her the name Orunamamu. She was teaching in the black studies program at Berkeley High School where some people objected to her family name, Washington, because George Washington was

1970s – 1980s

a slave owner. Besides, the rest of the black studies staff had African names. Don did some research and found "Orunamamu" which in the Yoruban tongue of Nigeria means, "Oh, you royal one, Miss Morning Star." They decided it suited her perfectly and she adopted the name.

She began her storytelling career in the 1970s while visiting Don in halfway houses where he was being treated for alcoholism. She developed a rapport with some of the other residents and, to cheer them up, told her father's old Army stories and tales she'd heard from her grandmother, plus others she'd collected over the years. Bit by bit she honed her craft until she knew she could hold any crowd. She began telling stories in schools and taught a class on the art of storytelling at Vista College in the 1980s.

She worked for the Berkeley Unified School District in various capacities for many years, but never received a permanent position. She officially retired in 1974 and continued to tell stories in Berkeley schools "without pay."

"Too stifling," she says of schools. "They are geared to maintaining the status quo. Schools often encourage controls on communication, and communication is the cause of nine out of ten problems we face in human relations. But," she adds, "I'm still a teacher. Once a teacher, always a teacher."

Her independent thinking has already incurred enough wrath from her "capitalistic, militarist" siblings. Yet she cares deeply about maintaining family ties, which is why, while she has often worshipped with the Quakers, she never joined the church. Her family didn't approve of the Quakers.

Connie (Carmella) Andersen, a long time friend and founder of Mighty Monday Mothers that meets on Tuesdays, tells me she met Orunamamu at a Quaker meeting in the 1970s. The group began gathering during the women's movement of that time for the sheer pleasure of sharing each other's company, and in the process, aired their concerns about the world as well as their personal issues. Orunamamu says the group fortified her emotionally through turbulent times, and now they are considering meeting on Wednesdays.

Orunamamu scraps, 1970s

Orunamamu still goes to storytelling conferences, though she's never a featured artist. That would entail writing resumés and getting photos and press packets together, which she just can't manage to do. Maybe if she understood modern technology or had someone to help her… but then it's not in the oral tradition to put things down on paper.

Traveling to festivals, traveling anywhere, her favorite form of transportation is Amtrak where she has the opportunity to tell stories. The conductor never stops her, glad of a diversion for the bored passengers, and she can really let loose on the train "because I'll never see those folks again!"

"Yellowlegs" is what she calls the home bought in 1969 when she was happily married to Jack. Piled everywhere, even on the front steps, are her "archives: scraps of paper stuffed into bags and trunks," one reporter wrote. He watched her "rummage around in one of several canvas bags she carries with her everywhere, bags filled with bag lady keepsakes like old books, yellowed newspaper clippings, bent photos, hand-written poems,

Orunamamu, 1997

train schedules, bits and pieces of stuff, every margin notated with addresses, phone numbers, directions, and stray thoughts."[1]

Orunamamu blames the inordinate mess on rebellion against her family's orderliness. Sometimes she can't even find Madame Ju-Ju, the corn snake she uses to teach about prejudice. "If you are prejudiced against black people or the Chinese, you need to learn the differences," she says. "I bring my snakes to show that most snakes are perfectly harmless and wonderful creatures. Just a few out of a hundred will be poisonous, and you need to learn which ones those are to avoid them." Then she gives her listeners a plastic snake to remind them and open their hearts.

Her dream is to turn her almost impassably cluttered house into a resource museum for storytellers. Her younger son Michael Santee, who lives in Oakland not far from his daughter Sasha and son Gabriel, keeps urging Orunamamu to either complete the project or throw out the trash.

Meantime, she "gets over," she says, somehow finding people to help her. "It's what I've always done." She usually sleeps on friends' couches, preferring companionship to privacy. She loves visiting her older son Eddie, a lawyer in Calgary, Canada who wants her to stay with his family six months every year rather than the three she does now. His son Omar, she says, is a musician in New York City and his daughter Sierra, a graduate of Harvard

Harvard Medical School, is at San Francisco General Hospital.

Orunamamu doesn't care that her work hasn't brought fame. She is happy to be one of the anonymous storytellers, once mostly men, who since ancient days have passed on wisdom and traditions from generation to generation.

Back on the street, she engages a young passerby in conversation. "I need to spread the word about stories. When you have a story, tell it to someone!"

[1]Howard Hinterthuer, *Porcupine*, 1991.

Postscript: *Orunamamu is wondering if there are any folks out there who are willing to help create a storytelling museum out of the treasures and trash scattered about her house. Write her at 5606 Ocean View Dr., Oakland, California 94618*

Orunamamu at home, 2005   *Photo: Amy Gorman*

Dorothy as an Indian Maiden, age 13. "My mother sewed all the feathers on the costume by hand."

"We just lived tap dancing. Didn't know what time of day it was sometimes."

The Asian Ginger Rogers
DOROTHY TAKAHASHI TOY
TAP DANCER
Born May 28, 1917

"We starved so we could dance.
We loved it so much we'd do anything just to keep dancing."

The Ginger Rogers of Asian American tap dance, Dorothy Toy along with her partner Paul Wing, the Chinese Fred Astaire, took the entertainment world of the 1930s and 1940s by storm, packing houses around the globe. From the Palace and Roxie on Broadway to the London Palladium, Toy and Wing were the first Asian Americans (called Orientals then) to enter the Caucasian American dance scene, and get bookings with the top big bands of the time.

Appearing on many TV shows, they reached a national audience on the Ed Sullivan Show. On the silver screen, they appeared in "Happiness Ahead," "Best Dishes," and "No Orchids for Miss Blanchard." Their Hollywood debut ended suddenly because of anti-Japanese sentiment, yet they opened doors for future Asian American dancers.

"I just had my 88th birthday," short, lithe, bright-eyed Dorothy exclaims as she invites me into her large, sunny Oakland home accompanied by three friendly yipping dogs. "Eighty-eight is a real lucky number for Chinese and Japanese. And that's eight, eight, double luck. It means long life or long good fortune.

"They gave me the biggest party you could imagine. My daughter came from France and my son came from Pennsylvania. Everyone was

1921 Dorothy and aunt

there. It was at Tommy Toy's, my nephew Alon Yu's restaurant in San Francisco. A real elegant place."

Dorothy's trim body is classily attired in tight black pants and black silk shirt, an orange scarf around her neck. Her hands may be arthritic, but her still-strong feet bounce energetically on stylish high heels.

Her contemporary home is a mix of Asian and American furnishings, an expansive Chinese carpet and sideboard, knickknacks from all over, a very American refrigerator plastered with photos and magnets with daily reminders. Framed publicity photos cover the walls, and on the dining room table is a large cardboard box crammed with yellowed newspaper clippings and more photos. Martial artist Mark Wong lives downstairs to help Dorothy keep her life organized – and the dogs walked.

Settling onto the living room couch, Dorothy launches into her past dance history with the speed of a chicken escaping from a fox. It's all I can do to keep up with her. She has just finished giving a two-hour dance lesson with two adult pupils, and her energy has not waned. She's ready for more.

She was born Dorothy Takahashi in San Francisco in 1917 to Japanese parents who had emigrated to the U.S. shortly after their marriage. From age seven, "I couldn't stop dancing. I danced on the sidewalk outside my family's restaurant, the Cherry Blossom Cafe in Los Angeles." The Cherry Blossom, which served both Chinese and American food (Japanese cuisine was almost unknown in the U.S. then), was across from the Regent, a vaudeville theater. "I used to watch all the acts, including my future partner, Paul Wing."

The Regent's manager spotted her dancing in front of the restaurant on her toes, ballet style, in her regular school shoes. He told Dorothy's mother she should have dance lessons. "We can't afford it," she said. Shortly afterwards, the manager sent over a teacher who also pleaded for Dorothy to have lessons, and again her mother said they couldn't afford it. The teacher offered to exchange meals at the cafe "for the privilege of teaching me dancing. And that's how I started."

In those days Asians did not take dance lessons. "But my mother was supportive and didn't listen to the older relatives who disapproved." So Dorothy was admitted to the Ransdell Dance School at the Conservatory of Music near Westlake Park in Los Angeles. She credits her teachers there for excellent instruction and the only formal lessons in acrobatics and ballet she ever had.

Dorothy first saw the Chinese Paul Wing dancing at Grauman's Chinese Theater in Hollywood. But she really got to know him at the family restaurant where he and the other performers gathered to eat regularly. They started dancing together and then decided to be a team, a trio, in fact, for her sister Helen joined them.

The girls took the name Toy, which was easier to remember and which fit better on a marquee than Takahashi.

In 1933 Paul and the sisters left for Chicago. Though the girls were still in their teens, their mother supported the decision. "She knew I had to dance, and they had no money. My sister and I didn't want to burden them with paying for us anymore." They hit the road, worked up routines, played small theaters and clubs all the way to the big time, Chicago. Once there, Paul and the Toy sisters realized they were five years behind the times. "We had to learn the latest tap steps, the modern close-to-the-floor work," Dorothy laughs. They learned fast. "We worked Chicago for about two years, in all those gangster night clubs."

That glitzy scene was no problem for two young girls, she asserts. "Nobody paid any attention. In those days people were so busy trying to make a living, everybody was so poor. And when you're

1922 Dorothy left, two cousins Ichiro and Sachicko

1936, First pro act with Paul Wing, Chicago

young, you can put up with just about anything. Nobody bothered us. People even took care of us because we were Asian, and they thought that was sweet."

It soon became clear that Helen was a better singer than dancer, and by getting separate gigs the sisters could each earn $17.50 per week, instead of splitting it three ways. So, while she and Helen sometimes still worked together, the Toy-Wing trio became a duo, and Dorothy and Paul Wing headed for fame.

It can't have been easy. Rusty Frank in her book *Tap* [1] writes: "Like their black counterparts, Asian American entertainers faced great prejudice in their attempts to have careers in the show business world. The general public had a difficult time believing that Asian Americans could sing and dance in the popular mode."

Frank adds that white prejudice was matched by that of the Asian community, "which traditionally looked down on the 'White Devils' world of shameless entertainment." Those who overcame the scorn of both communities were "remarkable people filled with drive, strength, courage and inspiration."

Dorothy only remembers the applause. "We opened in Chinese robes," she says. "After that it was all American, and we danced just like Ginger Rogers and Fred Astaire. The public wanted the other dances, too, which were in style in those days, like the Castle Rock." Their finale, a Russian number, always brought down the house. "I did all the Russian ballet steps en pointe. I had such strong feet I'd jump up in the air and land on my toes, in a plié. And my partner did 'legomania,' splits on the floor, trick stuff, all the things that sell. That's why no dance team could be like us."

In 1938, Toy and Wing were signed by the prestigious William Morris agency for a Broadway engagement at the Strand Theater. New York loved them. "We stopped the show completely! The people didn't stop clapping for us, and from then on it was fine." They played all the big circuits in the 1930s and 1940s, dancing at theaters that held 2,500- 5,000 people. They appeared with the top bands – Artie Shaw, Benny Goodman, Tony Pastor and Leo Reisman – often opening the show. "We just lived tap dancing," Dorothy recalls. "Didn't know what time of day it was sometimes. The other entertainers respected us because we were good."

So good, in fact, that in 1939 they were booked at the Palladium in London. Dorothy was nervous about performing there at first. "I didn't know if people would take to us or not because we were Asian." But soon they were doing four shows a

1932, The Three Mah Jongs: Dorothy, Paul, Helen (Leilani). First pro show. Courtesy of the Museum of Chinese in the Americas, N.Y.

1939, Hit the big time, New York

night and earning $2000 a week, even hired a driver to take them back and forth. People liked watching us because we were enjoying ourselves."

Then Hitler invaded Poland and World War II began. They were heading to the Palladium the night the blackouts began; their driver drove in the dark to get them there, for the show must… That Sunday they carried gas masks in church and heard sirens wailing. By Monday the British pound had dropped so drastically that their paychecks were worth only half. Despite the war, Toy and Wing continued dancing in London until leaving for a tour in Rio de Janeiro. Afterwards they returned to New York and a four-week engagement at the Paramount. Then America entered the war.

Dorothy and Paul were dancing at a New York club in 1940 when Walter Winchell, a popular columnist of the day, reported that one of the Toy-Wing duo was really Japanese. His headline was "Kicking Around the Gong," the title of one of their numbers. "He got mixed up which one of us was Japanese," says Dorothy. "But we didn't want the customers to come in and start throwing things at us, or for anything to happen to the club." The club owner shrugged it off. "Nothing's going to happen," he said, but he gave them permission to leave. They stayed away from New York a year, touring elsewhere, before returning to the Roxie.

About this time, Dorothy and Paul were asked to perform in a movie with a famous big band, and they packed up for the cross country trip. When they arrived in California they received a telegram canceling their contract because one of them was known to be of Japanese descent.

Meantime, Dorothy's parents were interned in Topaz, Utah. They urged their daughters to stay away from California, where persecution of the Japanese, citizens or not, was particularly bad. So, when Paul was called up for the army in 1945, the Toy sisters teamed up and got bookings in many Chicago nightclubs and in U.S. military camps.

Dorothy and Paul married during the war, but divorced after a few years. Their dance partnership continued long after their divorce. When Paul returned after the war, Toy-Wing resumed a heavy touring schedule. "And wouldn't you know it?" remembers Dorothy. "Walter Winchell then wrote: 'Orchids to Toy and Wing.'"

Dorothy met Lester Fong in 1950 while dancing at the Forbidden City, a popular Asian night club in San Francisco. From the late 1930s until the club closed in 1961, mainstream audiences flocked there to see the talented Chinese performers of Western-style dance. What the Cotton

1942, New York

Club was to Harlem in the 1920s and '30s, the Forbidden City was to San Francisco in the '40s and '50s. Toy and Wing were favorites there for many years.

After their marriage, Dorothy and Lester settled in the Bay Area, where their two children were born in the 1950s. Dorothy considered herself retired, at least from her heavy touring schedule, but she continued dancing with Paul Wing.

By the 1960s Toy and Wing realized that dance teams were out. The public was going in for revues – "for more nudity," as Dorothy puts it. Going with the times they produced shows featuring skimpily-clad young Asian Americans. Their Oriental Dolls Revue, one of the first Asian American revues, went on for four or five years. "Very hard to get good-looking dancers," she comments, pointing out photos of girls in feathers and fans.

"We played night clubs, then toured to Pittsburgh, Detroit, places like that. It sold very well, but it was hard to carry seven or eight people. I had to have Chinese costumes, Japanese costumes and American costumes. I supplied everything, all the shoes, stockings, everything. On the road the most important thing was to always make sure our costumes were with us."

Unfortunately, most of the costumes were lost during a move. "I don't know what happened to them. And you know, I had to pay $75 for the very first one. I worked ten weeks for that."

Raising children while touring, often for weeks at a time, was not a problem, Dorothy says. "My kids were quite easy to raise because show people are so nice. Lots of people took [them] so I could manage." In Reno, she went to a nearby Chinese restaurant and asked in a timid childlike voice if the owner had a daughter. She did, and Dorothy hired the girl to take seven-month-old Dorlie to the restaurant every morning and look after her for a couple of hours. "And nighttime – did I tell you about the stage manager who took her while I did the finale with Paul? When everyone's on stage, there's just one person left and that's the stage manager, so he took her."

When they moved to her present home in 1961, Dorothy added an apartment for her mother and sister Helen downstairs. "My mother and I spoke Japanese together," Dorothy recalls fondly. "And they helped a lot with the children. My sister was wonderful, never got angry – and she never married." Helen was working in the clubs and was gone most nights.

"That's also the time I had 60 Chinese dance students here. And we had a dance school in San Francisco that I started with four women partners. We taught hundreds of Chinese girls there."

Her divorce, after many years of marriage, must have been amicable, for Lester "used to come back here all the time." He moved to Los Angeles, where he got bit parts in movies. "He was nice, couldn't be nicer. Tall – handsome! We were best friends. His sister was Alice Fong Yu, the first Chinese teacher in the San Francisco public schools, who was a wonderful friend of mine.

"Lester opened a haberdashery, that's where he got such good clothes. But he loved to gamble. The horses. My mother felt so sorry for him she'd give him some money for the horses." He never could dance, she adds, and their son is just like him. "My son says he has two left feet," she laughs. But clearly she is very proud of Peter, a professor of Marine Biology at Gettysburg College in Pennsylvania.

Dorothy danced professionally until 1971, the same year her daughter

About her students: "I wouldn't miss them for anything. I live now to teach."

1982, Dorothy, Arthur Dong, filmmaker "Forbidden City;"
Rusty Frank, author, Tap

Dorlie, also a dancer, was Miss San Francisco Chinatown. For the next 25 years Dorothy worked as a pharmacy technician at San Francisco's Valencia Pharmacy, retiring at age 82.

Now she teaches dance in her downstairs studio, with sliding glass doors opening on the wooded backyard. Saturdays she has a class of high school girls, all Chinese American, and two women come "for fun" on Mondays. "They never miss a session, learn tap and ballet and have such a terrific time."

She wants to choreograph routines for her students, but they can't do difficult things like turns. Still, she says, "I wouldn't miss them for anything. I live now to teach."

After a lifetime of dancing, choreographing and producing shows, Dorothy has barely slowed down. She dedicates herself to putting on benefit fashion shows for non-profits including On Lok, the model San Francisco agency whose mission is to improve the medical and social lives of the frail elderly.

Her volunteer work has earned several awards, most notably from the Oakland Chamber of Commerce and from Family Bridges,

2002, Dorothy, Fayard Nicholas of Nicholas Brothers tap dancers, Rusty Frank

a senior community support center in Oakland's Chinatown. Honored for making outstanding contributions to the Asian community by WAVE (Women of Achievement, Vision and Excellence), an organization training young women for the work force, she proudly holds up a plaque and shows me the video.

Putting on a James M. Cohan tape of music from her heyday she starts tapping out a routine. She swirls elegantly around the room with a big smile on her face, and with eyes fixed forward she spins and spins. "I miss show business," she says, "but I wanted to end my career when I was on top."

Her career long over, she dances, as always, for love.

[1] Rusty Frank, *Tap*, De Capo Press, 1990

2005, 88th birthday with children Peter and Dorlie

Faith Craig, Whitman College, 1936

"With most songs, when I am singing them I am 'there,' wherever the song is, seeing and even participating in what's happening in the song. I would guess that many singers must do this and that it is the reason some close their eyes while performing."

The Fort Knox of Folk Music

FAITH CRAIG PETRIC

FOLK SINGER

Born September 13, 1915

"We sing of triumphs and tragedies, those of historic proportion and the small victories of daily existence. Indeed, it is almost only in folk songs that the flow of everyday lives – what people did, thought, felt – can be found."

Carrying on the great folk singing tradition of Woody Guthrie, the Almanac Singers, the Carter Family – she cut her first record in 1980 and four more followed. An international minstrel launched in her sixth decade, a third of a century of global touring and festivals, Faith Craig Petric is still a jet setter at 90.

Faith "doesn't make up songs, she harvests them," says the legendary singer/songwriter and storyteller U. Utah Phillips. "The outrageous and wonderful songs on her last CD," Utah continues, "culled from a bevy of extraordinary minds, represent those wild, satirical, quirky, offbeat and endearing traits that characterize the lady herself."

Nowadays Faith takes favorite songs, such as "Little Red Hen," "Amelia Earhart's Last Flight," and "Colorado Trail" ("my all-time favorite cowboy song – my almost all-time favorite song") to children's concerts, political rallies and folk gatherings. And, of course, there's "Geritol Gypsy" by Peter Krug, celebrating "a ramblin' renegade grandma, that's me!" Faith grins.

But she also loves the lyric, "There's no place that I'd rather be than right here," taken from a popular Country and Western song. "It seems important to me that I've been able to say that to myself many times and

Thornton, Washington. Faith, front left, 1927

places in my life."

She looks the part in her jeans and gray ponytail. Her ten-room, warm and worn, bright San Francisco Tudor-style home built in 1900, fits her perfectly. The entry bursts with bulletin boards covered with posters of local musical events, while mandolins, guitars and banjos adorn the high living room walls.

It's a far cry from the log cabin where she was born, on a homestead in northern Idaho near the Clearwater River. Faith can't remember a time when she wasn't singing, at home, in school or church.

"My father – a carpenter, farmer, inventor and Methodist minister – had a fine tenor voice. We had an old pump organ, and later a piano. With him I learned many treasured songs like, "Juanita," "Old Oaken Bucket" and "When You and I Were Young, Maggie."

Faith's mother, a school teacher since graduating from high school at 17, quit teaching after her marriage and the birth of five children. "She resumed when I was four and taught consistently until into her seventies." Faith recalls, "She wanted me to be musical and had me take piano lessons but I was never any good."

When she was nine, Faith and her brother Glenn discovered cowboy songs. A later favorite was Percy French's "Abdulla Bulbul Ameer." She says, "We used to act out the duel with swords made of lath."

At ten, her parents separated. Faith remained with her mother until high school when she lived for two years in a small boarding home. In her senior year, however, she rejoined her mother and brother in a small house in Moscow, Idaho. "It was the heart of the Depression, my mother couldn't find a school, and we did whatever odd jobs we could find to support ourselves."

In 1933 Faith went off to Whitman College in Washington. While working her way through school, "I sang in the glee club, and saw and played my first guitar."

In college she helped organize her first peace strike. The VFW, Veterans of Future Wars, were asking the government to pay their way through college now, not to wait for pensions until after another war that they might not live through. Faith and a friend arranged for speakers to come at 11am, the time of daily chapel, and about half of the student body of 400 showed up.

"They'd been lying to us," Faith says thinking back on her college days when she became radicalized. She'd been taught that America was noble, its elected representatives honest, working only for our good. "And then finding out it was all lies." For the political left, Washington was the most volatile state in the U.S. back then. It was known as the Soviet of Washington.

Inspired by Carl Sandburg when he gave a concert at Whitman College, she bought his song collection, *An American Songbag*. "He spoke my language," she says. "I've heard a quote of him saying rather than being remembered as a poet and historian, he would prefer to be remembered for his collecting and singing of old songs."

Faith and daughter Carol in Mexico, 1945

After college, Faith worked at a Seattle bookstore, then headed to San Francisco. She had plans to travel around the world but times were tough.

"I was so stirred… it inspired me to become a traveling musician. The whole thing fit me, my emotional needs, the way I could contact people."

She was lucky to land a job with the California Relief Administration. In 1939, a year later, she got a job she loved, with the Migratory Labor Program of the Farm Security Administration working with the dust bowl refugees. It was during those late 1930s that Faith found the great songs of the Spanish Civil War and radical, union, and topical tunes of all kinds; she was heartfully in the mix.

World War II canceled all hope of going around the world, but Faith, curious to see the other side of the country, took a job as a shipfitter at Todds Sun Shipbuilding in Hoboken, New Jersey. She was quickly drawn into the vibrant folk music scene in and around New York City. "I fell into the musical vortex around the company of performers like Josh White and Leadbelly. I couldn't get enough of the music and the energy."

Her daughter Carol was born in Mexico City in 1945. "Carol's father, Forrest Wilson, and I had planned to marry," Faith says, "but never got around to it." She returned to San Francisco a year later and in 1948 married her good friend Lubin Petric, and took his name. The marriage was brief and "spoiled a perfectly good friendship."

All along, she became more and more a freewheeling lefty, dedicated to anti-war, union and civil rights causes. Most of all she cherished the songs of working people. "From what is closest to the bone in their lives," she writes, "people of all tongues, times and regions have created folk song, instrumental music, stories, poems, drama and dance."

Through the McCarthy Era and the "Silent 50s," Faith raised her daughter, participated in PTA and, following her New Deal beginnings, worked for the California Department of Rehabilitation. Her emotional sustenance came from the community of the San Francisco Folk Club. Founded in 1948 by Dave Rothkop, it was reorganized in the 1950s by Herb Jager who gave it a more formal structure. He wanted to assure its continuity, so he promoted concerts and other benefit performances.

In the early 1960s, Herb asked Faith to take over the club's meeting schedule while he was gone for three months. He was gone for three years, so Faith "just kept on." New programs were initiated, such as jam sessions, group camping and the newsletter known as 'the folknik.' Since 1962, the bimonthly meetings have filled her home, which fast became an international mecca for folk musicians.

She bought the big gabled house at 885 Clayton Street in 1960 so her daughter could walk to Lowell, a quality high school in the city. To meet mortgage payments Faith rented rooms, selecting as tenants international college students.

In five rooms of her house during the 1960s, tunes melded and simmered, along with political, topical and social issues. There, folk musicians were jamming, singing, pairing, collating 'the folknik,' and writing new songs. Clayton Street rocked with music, from blues to bluegrass, country to swing, stoking the sounds of the latter decade Haight-Ashbury.

This was the place to go for folkies. Even in 2002 the San

IWW members at the Vancouver Folk Festival, taken July 15, 1979 Pictured left to right are: Che Greenwood, Al Grierson, Kate Wolf, Bruce (Utah) Phillips, Faith Petric, Fred Holstein, Tom Scribner, Dave Van Ronk, J B Freeman. Kneeling is Bodie Wagner.

Faith with Toshi Seeger in 1984

Francisco Chronicle reported that when Greg Jones got in a taxi with his guitar and asked to go to the Haight, the cabbie asked, "Going to Faith's?"

Meantime, Faith marched for civil rights in Selma, Alabama, protested the Vietnam War, helped to grow the San Francisco Folk Club as president, and performed around the Bay Area.

Then, in 1971, a year after retiring, her life dramatically shifted. She and three others while in the kitchen of her home, planted the seeds for what became "the Portable Folk Music Festival."

"We gathered fifteen people and a dog in an old school bus and toured the country." Audiences nationwide were entranced. One night after singing Utah Phillips' "Goodnight-Loving Trail," the first time it was heard in the East, Faith recalls that, "The audience remained quiet and then broke into enthusiastic applause. It was very moving… I was so stirred by the reception of the song, it inspired me to become a traveling musician. The whole thing fit me, my emotional needs, the way I could contact people." In other words, "I was bit by the bug – at 56!"

That moment launched her professional touring career. For the next three decades and more, she traveled the world, from Ireland to Australia, Katmandu to Malaysia, and all across the U.S.of A, Canada and back again. Sometimes sleeping in her car, sometimes on a plane – never mind – she was happy to be one of the legions of traveling players who for thousands of years have been the peoples' ambassador to a ruthless world.

At one time Faith pursued a goal of learning a song a day and often remembered a song, hearing it only once. Nowadays, before performing she carefully rehearses every song to be sure she's got the lyrics right.

"What songs and performing are to me is communication. I work to find and do what I think are the best ways to perform a given song so that it reaches the listeners: the phrasing, the emphasis, even the body language. With most songs, when I am singing them I am 'there,' wherever the song is, seeing and even participating in what's happening in the song. I would guess that many singers must do this and that it is the reason some close their eyes while performing."

But there are songs she's been unable to sing in public, because, "I feel something in them so deeply it makes me cry."

These days, Faith has cut down to a couple of shows a month and limits her travel to two or three months a year. Not that you'd notice from her plans for summer 2005: First to Hartford, Connecticut, where she received the Noam Chomsky award, then on to the Hudson River Revival and the Old Songs Festival in the northeast to perform, and finally back to the Oregon County Fair in July. "Then I'll travel with the Chautauqua Troupe in the Pacific northwest."

The folk gatherings at her house every other Friday night continue. Various groups and organizations gather at her house as well, including the Freedom Song Network, which she helped found in 1982.

Leading me to the third floor to find a copy of the song "She Was There" (written about her by Estelle Freedman), agile Faith gestures towards the vast library and music archives surrounding her computer and copy machine. She often spends her mornings corresponding, responding to queries, tending to SF Folk Club business, and writing a column for the quarterly "Sing Out!," the 55 year old magazine revered by folkies.

Touring England, 1986

An admitted labor-of-love-a-holic, one moment Faith says, "I'd like to give it all up, it's too much responsibility," and the next minute she says that her ego is too invested in the work she loves to drop any of it.

"The good news is you can get away with a lot more when you're old. You can be eccentric."

Faith has won many honors, including the California Traditional Music Society Award, the 2000 Labor Arts Award and the Joe Hill Award from the Labor Heritage Foundation in 2002. Then, at her 90th birthday celebration in 2005, Berkeley's Freight and Salvage gave her the key to their coffee house "for outstanding contribution to traditional music."

I feel a bit foolish asking how one can make sure old age is worth living. "It's not for sissies," she says. "You've heard that before, I'm sure, but it's very, very true.

"The worst thing is memory loss. I find it hard to cope with that. And I just don't have the energy I used to have. You rest more. Old age requires a lot of adapting.

"The good news," she adds, "is you can get away with a lot more when you're old. You can be eccentric."

When asked, Faith offers, "I believe in some form of spirituality," which she finds in songs. "And I like the line from Kurt Vonnegut's son that goes, 'We're here to help each other get through this thing, whatever it is.'" As to formal religious organizations, songwriter Iris Dement's "Let the Mystery Be" seems to sum it up for her.

At 90, Faith is as salty as ever, and still "protective, defensive, careful, closed," as she described her character of earlier years to an interviewer more than a decade ago.[1]

Her beloved granddaughter Alex, raised in Ireland and now 19, has moved in with her and often accompanies Faith to folk music festivals. She used to sing with Faith but is more likely these days to be stage managing.

Alex isn't her only contact with the next generation. "I get quite a following of younger people," Faith says. "They see this old woman getting up on the stage and singing fairly outrageous songs and radical stuff. They seem to like that."

But Faith has more to say to older people. "So often they'll say, 'Oh, you're my role model, I want to be just like you when I'm older.' And I say, 'No, you don't. You want to be just like yourself.'"

Though she seldom writes songs, she wrote this one for older people. The chorus goes:

"Life begins when you retire,
You're free to do as you desire.
You've paid your dues,
Now claim what's due.
Your life at last belongs to you."

[1]Estelle Freedman, *Oral History of Faith Petric*, Labor Archives and Research Center, San Francisco State University, 1992.

Faith at 89   *Photo: Amy Gorman*

Rosa Maria left, partner and teacher, 1943

"I always thought I would be dancing for the rest of my life; I just love to dance."

Viva la Song and la Swirl
ROSA MARIA MORALES ESCOBAR
SINGER, FOLKLORICO DANCER

Born December 25, 1923[1]

"I danced whenever I could. I had no idea what time it was when I was dancing."

Organist and musical arranger Solomon Guevara noticed Rosa Maria as a teen. Guevara was so captivated by her lovely voice he offered to train her for no money. Guevara's vocal coaching stood her in good stead later when friends prodded her to leave the dance floor and take the microphone as a volunteer singer at the Sweets Ballroom in Oakland, California, with bands like Benny Goodman, Cab Calloway, and Xavier Cougat.

Rosa Maria was a dancer, too. At the same Sweets Ballroom she participated in the *Tardiadas*, the Sunday afternoon Mexican dances organized by a promoter who brought the best bands of the day from Mexico. The place was jammed, and she never missed a Sunday. Rosa Maria recalls, "I always went with several girl friends chaperoned by one of our moms until someone's brother was old enough to take on the job. The mothers were happy to be relieved; they no longer wanted to accompany us girls to the dances.

"The fellas I hung around with always asked my permission if they could hold my hand. They were very polite." Those were the mores of her particular culture then, even when asking a girl to dance. "The way you behave is the way you're going to be treated. If you behave like a naughty girl you can expect the worst."

Rosa Maria is a warm, giving person, I see immediately on arriving for our interview. Her welcoming smile makes me feel right at home. "That's the plaque the Oakland Museum gave me when I talked to them about the city," she points out. It's especially important to her that such mementoes convey the rich history of Mexican-Americans in West Oakland. She proudly tells me her mother was the daughter of a Tarahumaran Indian who married a Spaniard, who came to Mexico during "one of those wars."

Costumes played a critical role in Rosa Maria's history long before she was born. Her father at 17 took his mother across the border to the U.S., then returned two weeks later for his fiancée, Rosa Maria's mother, and her mother (Rosa Maria's grandmother). He brought men's clothes for their escape from Mexico. "They dressed up as men and had the courage to do it," she says with gusto. "They traveled at night by burro, stagecoach and on foot for *ten months*, until they reached Chihuahua where they crossed from Juarez to El Paso sometime in 1915 or 1916. They paid three centavos to cross the border into El Paso, Texas."

Rosa Maria's parents came to California seeking a rosier economic future. Her dad, a towering 6'2" was an auto mechanic who filled the house with music – singing and playing guitar, drums, accordion and violin. Her mother, deaf in one ear, was very small, about 4'6". "When I climbed the Pyramid of the Sun in Mexico City I realized that many Mexicans were as tiny – you could see how small and narrow the steps were."

Her father learned English easily and became a citizen in 1925. But her mother, afraid she'd make a mistake on the test or not hear the judge, didn't become a citizen until

Rosa Maria, second from left, 1941

1940. Not that she wanted to, but she never returned to Mexico, saying Durango would be different from the way she left it and it would be too painful to see.

Rosa Maria, 1941

After three miscarriages, her mother gave birth to Rosita on Christmas Day, 1923, at their home on 8th and Filbert Street in Oakland, with the doctor in attendance. Both grandmothers also lived with them.

The grandmothers held jobs outside the home. Her maternal grandmother worked in the canneries of Del Monte, where she picked up Italian, the language of most of the workers. Her paternal grandmother commuted to Levi Strauss in San Francisco. "It took her three hours to get there! She left at 5 am, first hitchhiking from San Leandro Boulevard to Melrose. The truck drivers who picked her up sure got to know her. Then she took a train to the pier where a ferry took her across the Bay, and then a bus to the job." A gutsy woman, and yet no stranger to feminine arts, she also taught Rosa Maria to crochet.

Her family spoke Spanish at home so Rosita grew up in two cultures, and speaking both languages. She was nine when, after bouts of tuberculosis, pleurisy and pneumonia, her father died of strep throat – fatal in those days before antibiotics. Her mother, crippled with rheumatoid arthritis was unable to work, so applied for government assistance. They were faced with the indignities of the welfare system when their caseworker demanded to know why there were *more than two pieces of fruit on the table*: "You two are on welfare, you can only have enough for the two of you." Rosa Maria vowed she would never accept welfare as an adult.

Rosa Maria attended St. Mary's Catholic school in Oakland where there were other Mexican children enrolled, besides Portuguese, Irish and Italians. Then, she naturally applied to Holy Names High School run by nuns of the same order. She suffered another humiliation. The principal

Rosa Maria, center, 1944

saw her, bristled, and said, "Well, my dear, I think you have a lot of nerve coming here. Just look at the color of your skin. We have no room for you." [2]

At her pastor's urging she applied to St. Elizabeth's instead, where she received a scholarship, then went to Merritt Business College. Afterwards she worked as a secretary to support herself and her mother, and she laughs as she describes herself at the Oakland Shipyards typing memos that were presumably secret. "That's government for you. How can they be secret if I'm supposed to make fifteen copies!"

But dancing was always on Rosa Maria's mind. Still a teen, she danced with *baile folklorico* groups. "I couldn't wait to dance, any dance. I loved the groups and the feel of dancing to the music." Rosita was on her way to Sweets Ballroom December 7, 1941 when the news broke out that the U.S. was at war. All the cars and buses stopped, she says, and the people ran out of their homes.

She was working at the Army base during the war, and Rosa Maria was contemplating cutting her very long beautiful hair. At the time, the army needed un-permed hair to make bomb sites. After an officer asked Rosa Maria if she'd be willing to donate her hair to the army, she said yes, "I'll ask the barber to put it in a bag and I'll bring it to work." And that's what she did.

During World War II she often performed with the Mexican folkloric dance group, *El Caminito*, "the small road," organized through the YMCA. Her teacher, a Norwegian strangely enough, arranged numerous dance concerts for the Red Cross, for the *braceros* working in Oakland and at community centers. By then, immigrant laborers were arriving to work in the shipyards. "When Chilean and Peruvian ships docked at the Oakland piers, El Caminito Club sponsored dances and get-togethers for the

"I sang solo with all the bands… Boy did we have a good time!"

workers," Rosa Maria recalled. "I loved learning the Chilean dances, both *folkloric* and modern."

Looking back, Rosa Maria says, "I always thought I would be dancing for the rest of my life; I just love to dance."

She particularly enjoyed Salvador Guerrero's Latin American pop orchestra with whom she danced and sang for about five years. "I sang solo with all the bands he brought up from Mexico. He played all over Oakland and San Francisco in the dance halls. He played at Cooks Union Hall, at 11th and 12th and Clay Streets, and in the Oakland Auditorium. Boy, did we have a good time!"

She also danced at church fiestas most of her life. She will never forget the first one, at St. Mary's on 7th and Jefferson. It was there she met her husband, Fidel Rey Escobar, the bartender. "I don't drink," he told her, and she thought, "Oh yeah, that's a good line." He was from the St. Patrick's parish at 10th and Peralta, and had been a mail courier for the Army in India carrying mail and money over the mountains to Karachi. He wooed her by coming to hear her sing at St. Mary's. After singing she had to do her chores at the church. "Well, now I have to go and help the nuns," she'd say, and he'd say, "I'll go help too." He was constant. They were married 6 months later, January 31, 1948.

Fidel Rey Escobar

Rosa Maria, left, 1943

Rosa Maria, 1967

Fidel Rey Escobar worked at the Oakland Naval Supply Center from 1949 to 1976, preparing Army and Navy officers' cars for overseas shipment and inspecting them, especially for contraband. They raised four children together.

In 1966 Rosa Maria was approached to help start a Latino public library in the Fruitvale district of Oakland. "A Mexican lawyer called me and asked if I'd be interested in starting the library. I told him, 'Sure, anything to help the Latino community.' They presented a proposal to the State Librarian for $30,000 and got $300,000!" Today it is the Cesar Chavez Library, the East Bay resource for referencing all things Latin American.

Rosa Maria was their Assistant Director for ten years. "We weren't especially liked by the Oakland Public Library because we did a lot of unusual things. For example, we had taco sales in the library. And you could talk. I mean, you could come in and talk with your friends, or we would help you find information. We played bingo, had fashion shows and threw various holiday parties. Because there wasn't much material, we shopped everywhere, even ordered from Mexico." [2]

At the library, Rosa Maria wore many hats, including teacher of English to the Latino community, teacher of Spanish to the English-speaking community. The classes were always full. "I also translated brochures for places like Blue Cross, Kaiser Hospital, a Healthy Heart diet, and IBM."

And then there were the children. "There weren't any children's books in Spanish so I would read them the English books and [simultaneously] translate them into Spanish. I'd read ten books a week to them." She administered the facility, created programs, developed the materials, danced, sang and took on entirely too much. After three strokes in 1975-1976, though to change my diet completely."

But she continued giving to the community. When it came time to organize the Mexican festivals, Cinco de Mayo and Las Posadas, the Mexican procession at Christmas, Rosa Maria was right there. She and her husband danced at all the celebrations, jitterbugging, and dancing sambas, boleros, tangos, mambos.

Fidel Rey died in 1999, after 51 years of "a wonderful marriage." It was very difficult adjusting to the loss of her husband and favorite dance partner.

Today, Rosa Maria lives with her daughter in a comfortable ranch-style home in San Leandro in the East Bay. There are long lists of projects to upgrade the house, including painting it. "And I'm kept busy with my seven grandchildren and ten greats!"

She occupies herself knitting and crocheting for, as she says, "less fortunate people" in the community, with a group from St. Felicitas Catholic Church, which often meets at her house. Her living room is cluttered with large plastic bags of colored yarn, mostly pastels, donated by church members, and ready to be turned into shawls, scarves and baby clothes for rest homes and shelters. She derives pleasure from the handicraft itself, as well as from the emotional closeness of the group, women of Mexican, Filipino and Irish-Scotch heritage.

Creativity, she says, is a gift from God. One is born with it and God helps you use it. Rosa Maria feels lucky to have been born with the gift, and honored to have participated at so many wonderful events, especially those of the church.

Her serious singing ended 35 years ago when her vocal cords were scraped during thyroid surgery to remove a tumor. She currently enjoys singing in the choir, and for special occasions. But she speaks

Rosa Maria, 1980, singing at Library event

93

nostalgically of the days when she belted out her favorite Latin pop tunes, like "*Frenesi,*" (Frenzy), "*Solamente Una Vez*" (You Belong to my Heart) and "*Cuatro Vidas*" (Four Lives).

Arthritis has put a stop to her dancing days, too. But she delights in reminiscing about dancing *folklorico* as she pulls out photos of herself swirling in long multi-colored skirts. Then in her rich contralto Rosa Maria begins crooning the song still requested at all events, which she calls her theme song,

"*Vereda Tropical*" (Tropical Trail):

Haslo volver a mi
Make him return to me

Quiero besar su boca otra
I want to kiss his lips again and again,

Vez junto al mar.
Close to the sea.

Vereda Tropical.
Tropical Trail.

[1] Although Rosa Maria does not fit the over-85 criterion, by singing with the big bands, both Mexican and American, and dancing *folklorico,* she represents such a significant and colorful slice of Bay Area history that she is included in this book.

[2] "The History of Latinos in West Oakland: Community Narratives," Oakland Museum of California, 2000.

Rosa Maria, 82, at home

Grace with braided rugs, at 94

"I love to see a color combination or the way pieces of material fit together or not."

From Rags to Rugs
GRACE GILDERSLEEVE
RUG BRAIDER

Born November 25, 1911

"My favorite activity is to sit here in my kitchen working on my rugs while watching the birds and squirrels outside my window."

For over 25 years Grace has been braiding beautiful rugs, an art form she first learned at age 65. Now, at 93, she works on them a few hours every afternoon on the sturdy dining room table which overlooks her deck in woodsy North Berkeley.

Each rug takes at least a month, depending on the size. On her old rattling sewing machine Grace carefully stitches the ends of strips of material together. Then she forms them into an oval pattern and laces the strips together by hand.

She shows me a small worn red tin box and lovingly opens it, exposing buttons and pins of every size and color. "It was my grandmother's mother's" Grace says. "She may have used the same needle that I am using today. She was a ladies' tailor. The word 'seamstress,' was not invented at that time."

Her mother, she says, also made rugs using a large variety of mixed materials, but Grace is adamant about using only wool or wool-like blends. "I like the feel of wool, something soft. I don't like walking on cotton or any shiny material."

Her creative process unfolds as she selects fabrics with an artist's eye. "I love to see a color combination or the way pieces of material fit together or

Grace at 10

not." She tries one pattern, then another, waiting for just the right color and fabric mix to suit her. As she stands, then bends over as she searches for a special piece of cloth, I see her severe spinal curvature. It does not seem to interfere with her rug braiding.

Grace is well-named, for she is grace itself. Her positive attitude has carried her through many achingly painful times, including the early deaths of two children. She says her inner strength comes from having been greatly loved as a child.

Grace's childhood reads like a storybook about California in the early Twentieth Century. Her parents came from Illinois across the country by train in 1902 and Grace was born in Inglewood, near Los Angeles in 1911. Shortly afterwards she moved with her parents and two older sisters to Merced County, near Atwater where her family, the Cronks, had purchased 80 acres.

Her father, an artisan, carpenter and stone mason, had seized the opportunity to farm under a government land grant program designed to populate the empty farmlands of California. The family lived in a barn, the first thing Grace's father built on their new land. They raised almonds and peaches, the major crops of the area at that time, and Grace remembers her days on the farm fondly, painting a picture of her hard-working, skilled, optimistic and loving family.

"We learned to survive. We just thought this was living. We weren't poor – we just didn't have any money."

However, the family did own land, and Grace's generous dad donated two acres for a one-room schoolhouse. By the time the family left when Grace was 13, the school had expanded to two rooms with two teachers and some 50 students, plus a community room used by the neighborhood families in the evenings.

Grace feels discouraged about today's more affluent world. "I look back and I don't see anybody really any happier than my folks were, and they had financial troubles. But they had an attitude towards life... they were religious to begin with... but even so, they had an outlook that things were going to be better.

"They had no particular religion – they followed whichever pastor they liked at the time – they weren't fundamentalists who believe in hell and damnation. They didn't concern themselves with that at all... You never really heard them complain. They felt that life was good because they believed in God and that God would take care of them."

Grace remembers the hoboes coming from the railroad a mile away seeking work. "There was a class distinction. They were vagabonds, but most of them were not beggars. Most of them would work just for their meals. Some only wanted dinner, so would chop wood for an hour."

Her dad hired hoboes when he needed help, and let them sleep in the barn. When there were no hoboes around and they desperately needed workers, her mom would hitch up the one-horse buggy and hoist young Grace up beside her to go find one. And they always came home with a hobo. The buggy gave way to a car they purchased in 1918 when Grace was six.

Grace also remembers how homesick she was the summer she stayed with her grandmother while her mother was away. Most of all, she remembers the comforting hugs from her grandmother and great aunt. Right then she knew she was surrounded by good people, and always would be.

Despite their hard work, her parents lost the farm in 1924 when Grace was 13. "My memory is that my father had a feed and fuel store in Inglewood, and catered to

Grace, age 16, and mother

Grace married, 1936

chicken ranchers in the area. As the area became more urban the ranches disappeared, along with his business."

True to form, they picked themselves up and moved on, this time to Durham on Highway 99 with its still clear views of the Sierra Nevada. Her dad and a friend converted an old mill into a small chicken feed factory.

But what sustained them was the restaurant they started, "The Bark." With its hand-hewn manzanita tabletops and Mom's cooking, it became locally famous. Grace put in several years waitressing there.

In 1929 she went to the University of California, Berkeley where she discovered radical politics. "I majored in economics hoping it would land me a good job in the business world. I'm not sure if it was too hard or I just wasn't willing to put in the effort to master the subject. If I have any regret, it is that I didn't pursue a degree in history, which I loved. I remember everything I ever learned in those [history] classes."

Unable to figure out a major that both interested her and would help her earn a living, she dropped out after two years. She married a librarian for the State of California who shared her interest in radical politics. In 1938 they moved to Sacramento and settled down to raise their three sons and daughter. She helped him accumulate a collection of progressive posters and flyers now archived in the State Library.

Grace and her family moved from Sacramento to El Cerrito and then, in 1953, to Berkeley. Family life in her thirties and forties was more or less ordinary – until tragedy struck.

In 1960, their second son Joel, only sixteen, died of Hodgkin's disease. In 1968, her oldest son Stephen died at age 28 from an overdose of drugs, leaving a wife and two young daughters.

"...I can concentrate for hours when I'm making the rugs."

"Their deaths left me angry and numb. I just lived day by day," she says. "You have to not think about too many things... *Turn that off*. Otherwise, it's too many things in ninety years... you don't want to remember them all." She pauses for a while, "which has nothing to do with making rugs!"

Grace was livid at the system that so easily permitted the drug culture. She considers herself today "best friends" with Stephen's widow, Larkie, and very close to her granddaughters, although none of them lives in California.

After her husband retired in 1977, they moved to Fort Bragg on the wild northern coast of California, where he had inherited a house. There she learned the craft of rug-making from a master artisan named Virginia, a close friend of her mother-in-law.

Grace bought old clothes at thrift shops and got started. What intrigued her at first were the beautiful linings of the jackets and coats. "I tried making little things with them, but I soon lost interest in them." She wanted to make rugs.

When her husband John died in 1988 Grace moved back to Berkeley, to their former home in the hills. Her son John ("Ike") and his wife Patti and their family had made it their home since Grace went to Fort Bragg, and now they created an apartment for her downstairs. It became a three-generational home.

Once settled, "I quickly became active in the campaign to

Grace with sons Ike, Joel and Stephen, 1950

101

re-elect Ron Dellums to Congress. I felt like a crusader, going from door to door, saying 'You *have* to vote for this man!'"

All along she made rugs, experimenting with different patterns and colors. It became the part of her life that never left her. She says that now, in 2005, her mind wanders when she reads. She just can't stay with the page for very long. "But I can concentrate for hours when I'm making the rugs."

While rug making brings inner peace, her view of the world is more pessimistic than ever before. Politically, she says, she has never seen things so bad. She fears that big corporations will soon run the world, and that our current political system will no longer work well.

"After the Vietnam War," she says, "you thought you had taken care of war. You thought this country had learned about war. Well, they hadn't. What this country has learned is greed, and the desire for power is something you can't cope with. Greed goes along with power and power goes along with greed. I don't know which is which." She pauses, then adds, "And that's why I work with my hands."

Grace with husband John and two grandchildren, 1977

When asked if she is ever hopeful, she replies, "Oh yes, I get a lot of junk mail from many good causes, and I respond to some of them although I cannot respond to all. I see so many people working towards a common good."

Powerful in her ideas, outspoken in her beliefs, it is the gentle expressions of deeply felt emotion that so touch me: the smile she smiles when a guest arrives, her inquiries and interest in your own story. I hear the small sigh when she says her life is shrinking but she can't complain because she really has everything she could possibly want right here in this house.

Hard of hearing, Grace refuses to wear a hearing aid because, she says, the feedback is too great. Her hearing loss is limiting, keeping her home most of the time. "I really prefer the quiet, or to talk with someone here. I even had to give up the Unitarian Church which I went to for years and years.

"Until a couple of years ago, I met with some friends every month. Now I have very few that I speak to. We just faded away from each other. It just became too cumbersome to visit, especially the transportation."

Grace and daughter Cornelia, 1985

Something she can do easily is talk with people at home or on the telephone. She loves company and speaking with her many relatives on the phone, especially her daughter Cornelia who lives in Victoria, Canada. Grace only wishes she could see her more often, but finds it too hard to travel.

Suddenly her eyes light up. "What has happened," she says, "is that I have developed several new friends that I share time and stories with on a regular basis. At my age I am surprised and thoroughly delighted with this turn of events. I really like these times, especially since they come visit me here at home."

Despite friendly visits and a loving family, Grace's social life is curtailed. She sees it as part of her aging process, and finds quiet joys in watching the birds and squirrels from her patio. But her greatest pleasure is making rugs from the bags of clothes her family brings from thrift shops. Pleated skirts are her favorite finds.

She gives the rugs to all her family members, and friends of theirs who ask her. Most are oval, small ones from about three feet by two feet to great big ones of close to ten feet long. They range in color from various brown-black fabrics to bright greens mixed with blues. Finding the right color matches is a special joy for Grace.

Grace glows, reflecting on her ninetieth birthday party at the Unitarian Church. She lists all her family members who came to be with her from around the country. The family roles are reversed now, and her children and her six "grands" and four "greats" make sure she is well taken care of.

Grace revels in the love the members of her family have for one another. She sees her father's hands in her son's. Grace's father, Grace herself, her son and now his three sons – the gifted hands have come down through the generations.

Grace and rugs, 2004   *Photo: Greg Young*

Grace, age 91

Photo: Paula Eidson

Elsie demonstrating ikebana, 1960

"That's how much I like flowers," she says. "I want to be remembered for designing flowers. I drive all the way here from Vallejo and don't even get tired."

The Art of Arranging
ELSIE OGATA

IKEBANA ARTIST

Born August 20, 1912

"I had a good teacher, and that's how I learned."

Elsie has demonstrated ikebana, the art of Japanese flower arranging, around the Bay Area for decades. Walking through aisles of orchids, mums, roses, iris and mixed bouquets, I meet her in the back room of Adachi's, her family's flower shop, where she is making a gardenia corsage for a St. Patrick's Day celebration. It's a busy time for her. As she works, she instructs her young assistant, sometimes in English, sometimes in Japanese. Elsie moves easily between the two worlds.

She has helped coordinate workshops and the annual floral design shows at Golden Gate Park, and created floral arrangements for hotels and conferences. She says, "Depending on the situation, you can have formal or freestyle arrangements." She still works at Adachi's two days each week, in El Sobrante, California.

Elsie learned ikenobo, a form of ikebana back in her high school days. Her father would drive her and one of her sisters from their home in Richmond, California to Mr. Baba, their teacher at the Berkeley Buddhist Church. "My father wanted us to be good little ladies, good Japanese wives, and that included being skilled in flower arranging. My father believed that ladies were supposed to be cultured… We studied for years and years."

At 90, Elsie is spry and wears a sporty beige pants suit. She walks

Elsie at 15

briskly, with focused determination. Always smiling, she pays attention to her work while she puts me at ease.

She looks up at me tentatively (she's eight inches shorter than my 5'7"), as if wondering how to convey to this stranger her long and complicated life. First, she shows me how to wrap the tape around the corsage. Then, continuing to work on an arrangement, she talks in a matter-of-fact voice.

Although born at home in Richmond, California she lived in Japan with her grandmother, an esteemed music teacher, until she was 12. Her parents and siblings lived in California, and when her grandmother died Elsie's mother brought her back to California to live with them in Richmond. "My mother was a very refined person," Elsie says proudly. "She had exquisite taste, loved fine clothes, music, flowers and expensive art."

But it was her father who took charge of Elsie's education. To make sure she mastered English, he took a very unusual course of action: he enrolled his young teen-aged daughter in first grade for a year before she entered Richmond High School.

She went on to U.C. Berkeley and graduated in 1939. Elsie then returned to Japan with plans to write a book on nutrition, her field of study. While living there with her uncle, an obstetrician/gynecologist, World War II broke out. Although the U.S. State Department sent a warning for all its citizens to leave, Elsie ignored it.

Her family in California was interned and she scarcely kept in touch with them; she was allowed to send them only one card a week. Her

Elsie, about 1932

Elsie with relatives of Chiura Obata in Japan, 1940 before the gardens were bombed and burned

father, caught with a short wave radio, was sent to the more severe internment camp in Bismarck, North Dakota, while her mother and siblings went to Topaz, Utah where many families went and stayed together. Elsie still doesn't know what their lives were like then, for they never talked about it. They were silent when queried. Rather than being grateful that she was not sent to the camps, she has always felt distanced from her family because she did not share their experience.

While in Japan, she married Toshio Kano and had two daughters. She named them Betty and Susan, "the simplest American names I knew." Life was a struggle in the north of Japan with its bitter winters and the privations the war had brought. Elsie worked hard at unaccustomed domestic chores like hauling water, to get her family through that time.

Finally, in 1949, she returned to the U.S. with her family where her husband attended U.C. Berkeley. Afterwards, he received a scholarship for graduate studies at Harvard University. She was overjoyed to be reunited with her family in the U.S., but faced a difficult choice: whether or not to stay in America after her husband's two years at Harvard (1952-1954). She leaned toward staying, but Toshio resented American prejudice against the Japanese. They were still trying to decide what to do when, in 1956, Toshio died from a heart attack while diving for abalone on the California coast.

Elsie in best coat, 1942

1947, Matzushima near Sendai, Japan with father, his sister and grandmother. Elsie sits with daughters Betty and Susan on her lap.

Elsie stayed in California working long hours at the family business to support her daughters. Somehow, Adachi's survived the war despite having its windows smashed, and being looted while the owners were interned. In the following decades, it became one of the best-known flower shops in the East Bay region. It has moved several times since then, and today is much smaller, but it still provides employment for the family. "The men run the business and own the lion's share," says Elsie, "but the women do the flower arrangements."

Susan, Elsie's second daughter, supplements the family history. "Our grandfather started the nursery. He had built greenhouses… and had prize-winning roses. He was about 40 when he sent away for a picture bride. It was my grandmother, and she was 18, a classical situation." She continues, "Flowers are good – you always need them. It's like food, spiritual food, nourishment for the soul. Flowers are like the medium between the seen and the unseen worlds."

Elsie met her second husband Dye Ogata, a family acquaintance, during the 1950s at the flower shop. When they married in 1969, Elsie had been a widow for 13 years. Elsie and Dye spent ten years in Canada and the next 15 in El Cerrito, enjoying an active social life filled with sushi parties and church gatherings. Then, several years ago, Dye said it was time to sell their house and go to an assisted living facility in Vallejo. Elsie fought the move furiously, but finally gave in. It doesn't bother her that they are the only Japanese people there, but she misses her old friends and she hates the food. She always looks forward to eating out.

She still drives to her job in El Sobrante where she works two days each week. "That's how much I like flowers," she says. "I want to be remembered for designing flowers. I drive all the way here from Vallejo and don't even get tired."

She was honored recently as U.C. Berkeley's oldest Japanese woman graduate at a luncheon given by Japanese women alumni. Both her daughters attended that University, she mentions with pride, and two grandchildren are currently enrolled there. Another granddaughter attends M.I.T.

Elsie can't tell me what inspires her creative process. She says she was born with a talent; that her strong early training in ikebana has enabled her to develop into art. "Ikebana work takes a long time. It's long, hard, dirty work, and it's a long time before you can get to this," she says, pointing to an arrangement.

Finishing a sparse decorative bouquet she remarks, "This is a nice container. I don't think I'll put too much into it. Two is too much, and one is not enough." She laughs. "And the vases have to be artistic."

> *"Two is too much, and one is not enough. And the vases have to be artistic."*

Elsie doubts that the present generation will follow in her footsteps. "They don't have that kind of interest. They do computers, etc. They're doing okay, but we have to make this place okay too."

Elsie's daughters, Betty and Susan Kano, are aware that their mother forgets names, events and time sequences. They accept this as part of the aging process and are grateful that Elsie carries her years so well, remaining active and involved in her art. They honor her because her advanced age not only makes her wise, but as an elder she is closer to God.

Elsie herself believes in preparing for the body's deterioration by learning to do many different things. When she is not arranging flowers, her hands are busy at needlepoint and quilting.

But just now, she has to finish her St. Patrick's Day arrangement.

Postscript: *This piece was written in 2004 several weeks prior to Mother's Day when Elsie suffered from a blood clot in her brain. She endured surgery and a long recuperation period. Today in March, 2006 she is healthy and fully functioning. It is a testament to her strength and vitality that she is as cheerful as ever and still arranging flowers twice weekly at Adachi's.*

Elsie at Adachi's, 1999

Elsie, Betty, Malcolm, 2004

Dye, Joshua, Rhonda, Betty, Elsie, Naomi, 2001

Stella Toogood at 28, England, 1942

"When I was doing the radio show, I would have children in the studio
and engage them in conversation. I would ask how old they were and they
would hold up their fingers. 'This is radio!' I had to tell them."

Tales from Bristol to Berkeley
STELLA TOOGOOD COPE
STORYTELLER
May 9, 1914 – August 1, 2004

"If you're a storyteller, you can read a story and know that that's your story. You don't try to tell one that isn't your story."

Stella Toogood enchanted generations of young listeners with her storytelling. Her "Tell Me Again Tales" ran on Berkeley's KPFA radio for eight years in the late 1950s and 1960s, and she continued to spin tales in the Berkeley public schools until her death in 2004.

It is 2003, and Stella at age 88 wears pink sweater that enhances her white hair, gentle voice and melting smile. Her last name is apt. Toogood is old Anglo-Saxon, she says, going back at least to her grandfather, a founder of the Carpenter's Union in Bristol, England.

Her gracious offer of a "cuppa tea" is another reminder of Stella's English roots. Putting a worn cozy on the cracked teapot, she asks if I prefer English crème or tea biscuits. Stella clearly has a history with tea. I sink into a dining room chair feeling well taken care of, and her cat "Kitty" snuggles up on my lap.

Her love of stories began as a child back in Bristol. "My mother was a natural storyteller. She was a literary person and made up stories for us as children, serial tales that went on every night at bedtime. We had a different episode each night."

Her mother had to leave school at fourteen but read voraciously all her life. At the dinner table she talked about books like *Vanity Fair* and

Stella at KPFA studio, Berkeley, CA, 1955   *Courtesy of KPFA*

Barchester Towers, and interested the children in the characters. She often joined in their make-believe games.

There was no television or even radio when Stella was very young, but she calls hers a rich, indeed timeless, upbringing. "The way we entertained ourselves was either to read or tell a story. It was just a natural thing. We thought that was the way you did it."

When the time came for Stella to go to kindergarten, she was ill. Her parents suggested she take the whole year off to learn at home in the family environment, an appealing idea to a five-year-old-girl. "My eyes lit up," recalls Stella. "I learned to read in two weeks!"

Stella's father, too, played a huge role in shaping her life, his knack for words sparking her love of language. "Don't be a gongapooch!" he'd say when Stella looked disgruntled. She smiles affectionately as she remembers this.

Her father, who worked in an airplane factory and was an active trade unionist, gave Stella her lifelong dedication to working peoples' causes. Though a pacifist in World War I, he chose to continue working in the airplane factory in order to stay near his family, rather than follow his principles as a conscientious objector.

She remembers as a child helping with the work for the miners' strike. "My father got his fellow workers to donate tools for sale to give money to the miners in South Wales. Whenever we'd have an election, we would go around chalking on the pavements and walls for a candidate, you know, put slogans out. We used to love to do that as children."

Political talk, discussions at home around the dining room table –
there was always an open verbal back and forth, which stimulated her.
"Children were not excluded from conversation in my home," Stella recalls
with pride.

Her sister Pauline (Pauline Cutress) lives in England but visits often,
and we met on several occasions. Fifteen years younger than Stella, she
vividly recalls making puppets with her. Their father made them a portable
theater, and they went around giving puppet shows. Pauline especially
remembers the Christmas they went to an asylum for the "mentally
deficient" where they performed for groups of inmates. The last group were
the "morally deficient" – teenagers locked up because they were pregnant
and unmarried.

"Were they happy to see us! Afterwards we had tea with them and
did country dancing." Pauline will never forget the circle dance with arms
linked around each other's waists whirling in joyful excitement. For the
girls, she recalls, it was a pleasure just to be with people from the outside.
Stella continued giving puppet shows well into her sixties.

Her family had little money for her father earned minimal wages.
"Mother was supporting
my father (in his political
activities) and believed what
he was doing was right."
Luckily, he loved gardening
and raised chickens and
ducks, so "we had our own
eggs and vegetables and a
decent standard of life."

But there was
no money for Stella's
education. "At that time you
had to pay a lot of money

Esperanto party, 1982 with Dr. Zamenhof. Stella, 68, is second from rt.

Stella teaching Esperanto, 1983

to go to high school." Fortunately Stella got a scholarship to a prestigious boarding school, then to a teacher's college, the Fishponds Diocesan Training College. She felt privileged to have such good training, although she was critical of the rote learning methods, with little room for individuality.

Stella began telling stories as a grade school teacher in Bristol just before World War II. She spent her leisure hours at the Folkhouse, where she loved to folk dance, sing, hike and bike around the countryside.

The Folkhouse then was an important movement in northern Europe, especially in Holland, Norway, Denmark and England, where it was funded by the Workers Education Association and the churches. Its aims were to provide continuing education and to build community. The classes in many varied subjects were taught at a very high level, and attracted those lacking a secondary education as well as educated middle class students.

A Folkhouse instructor invited Stella to take his class in Esperanto, the artificial language designed to be the universal tongue. She did so reluctantly but quickly fell in love with the language, which represented her ideal of breaking down cultural barriers between peoples. She became proficient and went on to teach Esperanto, first in England and later in the U.S.

By now World War II was looming. Stella was attending a meeting of Esperantists at a Folkhouse camp in Denmark when the police rushed in and arrested the photographer taking pictures of the proceedings. He was a German spy.

While she was attending another meeting in 1939, the Germans invaded Denmark. She was hustled onto the last boat to leave for England, packed with panicky refugees.

World War II was a dismal time for Stella, as for everyone. She recalls the air raids as being particularly awful. What made things worse for her was her pacifism. It was a wrenching dilemma trying to hold to her pacifist principles in the face of the German atrocities. Stella struggled over participating in school tasks to assist the war effort, but knew she had no option. She was trapped between her conscience and the realities of war.

Meanwhile, she had nearly fifty frightened students to handle under difficult physical conditions with no help. "Some people were very successful at handling that situation. I found I wasn't, really. The only thing I could do was to use my storytelling to back up my classroom teaching."

One thing she could do in all good conscience. With fellow members of the Bristol Friends Meeting she took on fire watch duty. When she was able to join her family in the bomb shelters, there were, as always, stories to tell – some imagined and some very real.

After the war, a young American man invited her to come to the U.S. It was hard leaving England and her family, but Stella, feeling stifled in her job, knew she had to. Although that friendship did not last, opportunities – unavailable in England – opened up in the U.S.A.

California in 1947 after post-war England "was like a paradise," she recalls. "This kind of freedom to maneuver was a tremendous experience for me… it was a new world and I felt anything was possible."

Struggling with American idioms at first – "I made some funny mistakes, like going in to ask for 'grips' instead of bobby pins" – she landed teaching jobs, first in Palo Alto and then in San Francisco. Finally, settling at the Girtan Childcare Center at U.C. Berkeley, she also took

Stella and Calvin, 1991 (77 and 94 years)

Stella in 1996 with Japanese friend

classes at the University. She loved both working and going to school. "At that time in Berkeley – unlike these days – you could live on a very modest income and have some decent housing."

Meantime, she attended the monthly meetings of the Esperantists Society and several of their annual conferences. But what brought her to Berkeley's attention was the Kiddie Korral, a day care program she started at the then new Berkeley Co-op supermarket.

Word got around that Stella kept kids spellbound with her stories. And Bob Schutz, director of KPFA, whom she knew from Quaker meetings, invited her to tell her stories to their radio audience. "In the late 1950s", she says, "KPFA was much more inventive, experimental and informal" than now.

The thought of talking on radio was terrifying. "I was so nervous about it, we didn't do it live. I made a tape which they replayed, and they did that for a few weeks. And I realized that somehow it didn't touch me off." So she invited children to come into the studio. "It made the story so much more alive to have children there." She quickly became a hit with young listeners, and her half-hour show, "Tell Me Again Tales," went on to air twice weekly for eight years.

She scoured libraries for stories she could make her own, borrowing from Beatrix Potter, African tales of the trickster *Anansi the Spider* (akin to Coyote or Br'er Rabbit), popular books like *Ferdinand the Bull*, and *The White Cat that had Black Kittens*, which was banned in the South. This was 1958. She chose her stories not only for their entertainment value but for their messages. They resonated with many children, some of whom corresponded with her for years.

Stella is still grateful that KPFA let her choose her own stories and tell them in her own gentle way. "If you know children, you know what appeals to them. But it has to be a story you enjoy yourself and would enjoy telling," she says. "And of course every time you tell a story it changes… and the children you tell it to help it to change a little."

Thanks to the radio show, more people came to the Kiddie Korral at the Co-op. Vangie Buell (then Vangie Elkins), who worked with her at the Co-op, calls Stella her mentor. "Children listened intently to her. Her voice had such a beautiful resonance. She acted things out, like bringing her hands to her ears for bunnies. She was radiant."

When Stella and several of her co-workers were told to split their shifts at the store, Stella drafted a proposal to management explaining why they refused. She also asked for pay raises, sick leave and vacation. Stella was indeed her father's daughter.

The Co-op manager's response, Vangie recalls, was something like, "You girls belong at home with your babies and how dare you make these unreasonable demands." He soon faced an outraged red-faced Stella.

Union representation was not far behind. Vangie states, "We won our proposals and became the charter members of the Union for the Kiddie Korral, Office and Technical Employees Union Local 29."

Stella, 1996 with Katherine Whittaker and Connie Andersen

During this period, Stella also worked for Oakland Head Start, and was a volunteer teacher for the Hopi Indians. What's more, she taught adult education classes at the San Francisco jail. That took some doing. First, as leader of the group, she had to convince the San Francisco Sheriff. "I had to talk to him week by week to tell him what plans we were making, things that he liked or didn't like."

Finally, they got permission to start a carpentry class. "We did have to check the tools carefully at the end of that day," she admits, but "the men were such wonderful people. They were so glad to have us come in. It sort of broke up the monotony of their day." Since participation was voluntary, they tended to get the more intelligent prisoners. Later, she taught reading and literature classes.

> *"The way we entertained ourselves was either to read or tell a story… that was the way you did it."*

Stella was required to have a male escort to go to the jail. On the way there one day the car broke down. "Stay in the car," he ordered as he went to phone for help. But as soon as his back was turned, she got out. Sometimes an attitude of independence can pay off. Minutes later another car smashed into theirs!

Stella applied for citizenship, but being an activist created difficulties, and she was investigated by the FBI. Jessica Mitford, the legendary British writer and activist, stepped in to help Stella achieve her goal.

"Saluton, amiko," said Calvin Cope when they met in 1976, through Servas, an international organization of hosts and travelers. Stella had often been courted, but not by a retired professor (17 years older) who said "Greetings, friend," in Esperanto. At age 67, in 1981, she entered married life.

Stella and Calvin spent 15 years together in their north Berkeley home sharing friends, Quaker beliefs and mutual interests in the cultures of the world, until Calvin was diagnosed with Alzheimer's disease. In the hard years of caretaking until his death in 1996, Stella was grateful for the help of several Chinese students who lived with them, especially Mingchi, now Mingchi Carroll, one of the first of Stella's Chinese friends and a fellow Esperantist. They continue to maintain close connections.

Stella lives in the same home she shared with Calvin surrounded by books, tapestries, music and wall hangings from around the world, all comfortably aged. Relishing a late morning breakfast, she peers into her garden through the sunny kitchen window and remembers so many stories.

"When I was doing the radio show," she reminisces, "I would have children in the studio and engage them in conversation. I would ask how old they were and they would hold up their fingers. 'This is radio!' I had to tell them."

Stella is often invited to meet with other storytellers seeking her advice. She supports and guides them, though she herself was never one to show off her skills at storytelling conferences and festivals. Twice a month she tells stories in the Berkeley public schools. She devotes one day

2000, reading a poem to Connie Andersen on Connie's 80th birthday

Stella, almost 90, telling stories in a Berkeley classroom

a week to the Gray Panthers, an advocacy group for elders. She sings in the choir and is an active board member of the Friends Church, which has been her central spiritual force since her twenties.

Nowadays, her Chinese tenants help with the chores, but having no family, Stella is mostly on her own. Transportation is the biggest problem. "It's not easy finding people to drive me, and since it takes two buses to arrive at many of the places I go, I occasionally must forego something. It's not easy for me to do that."

Stella attributes her longevity in part to the early love and guidance she received from her parents, particularly the advice to learn to support herself and never take anything for granted. Stella had to make her own tough decisions and, looking back, she says she'd still make the same choices.

Joe Brennan, now a family friend, recalls being entranced as a boy by Stella's show. "She used to mimic many different voices, use a deep Moglie voice (the Kipling character), then a high pitched one." He remembers her being "always optimistic and cheerful. She seemed immune from the darker things."

Another lifelong admirer is Mike Kirk, a boyfriend back in 1947, when they were students at UC Berkeley. They rekindled their romance some years later, but it was temporary, Joe says.

But just now, in 2003, Stella isn't thinking of bygone days – she's telling a tale about *Anansi the Spider*. "He's quite a little hero in West Africa and the West Indies. A funny little fellow, sometimes he can be a real person, but when in danger he becomes a spider.

And he's very whimsical; he's very naughty and mischievous, plays tricks on people. He can also get the best of big animals like Tiger and Lion and Snake…"

She smiles as if sharing a secret with a child. "He always comes out the best."

Postscript: *An archive of Stella's stories and the children's books that inspired them is kept at the Friends Meeting House on Vine Street in Berkeley, California.*

Stella at 88   *Photo: Paula Eidson*

Madeline at 100

Photo: Courtesy of Oakland Tribune

"What I believe is, treat people as you would like to be treated, not as people treat you."

Oh, You Beautiful Doll!
MADELINE MASON
DOLL MAKER, SCULPTOR

Born April 20, 1902

"I just do it. I see something, I like it and I just do it."

A sculptor and doll maker, the feisty Madeline lives in her Oakland home along with many of her creations. The clay heads, plaster people and rag dolls lend a lively atmosphere, and create warm surroundings.

A tiny person, not more than 4' 8" and eighty-five pounds, Madeline greets me at her front door in 2004 with a huge grin and a hearty "Hello, pleased to meet you, come right in." I feel right at home. She walks assuredly, assisted by a cane. Although she speaks easily, it's sometimes difficult to understand her, for she slurs some words. She tells me proudly that her birthday is coming up. "On April 20, I'll be 102. I have the same birthday as Hitler, and he didn't like blacks or Jews!" She laughs.

Madeline moved from the East Coast to California in the late 1960s to be near her daughter, Clara. Shortly thereafter, in her late sixties, her creative passions ignited when she discovered Laney College and its legendary art department. Madeline had always liked crafts projects, and gravitated towards working with her hands. She smiles, remembering as a kid creating balls of all sizes out of pretty paper and, as a teen, ransacking the library for books on hobbies to get ideas for things to make.

But creating art had never been a burning desire until Laney. Once there, she worked with clay, making small sculptural pieces. She made

Nursing school graduation. Madeline is bottom row, third from the left, about 1926.

heads. She loved the process of doing the work. She kept going back for more and more classes until she was well into her eighties. Her grand-daughter Nkenge reminds her that she was the oldest in the class by then. Madeline took Nkenge to class with her for several summers, for she enjoys passing on her artistic know-how.

At Laney she found that the medium of plaster intrigued her. She played with it for a while until huge, larger-than-life-sized plaster dolls emerged which she painted colorfully. Brown faces, pigtails, blue silky skirts, jeans on one. Two of those dolls now decorate the outside of her house sitting contentedly in the green grass. The dolls were far too heavy for one person to manage so she needed help to move them, and truck them to her house.

Madeline shows me the collection of clay pieces scattered around her compact house. Asked how she conceives of making a piece – what her artistic process is – Madeline says, "I just do it. I don't think about it. I see something, I like it and I do it." One day she saw a stuffed, hand-made doll and thought, "I can make that."

She started sewing ornamental pillows of gingham and colorful patterns to prepare her for the doll project. Then she bought material, constructed a doll, liked it and thought, "I'm going to make some more."

She made dozens over the next several years, many large, almost life-sized stuffed dolls. She thinks she sold several and gave the others to relatives and friends.

Madeline's prolific doll-making and sculptural output led to a retrospective of her work in 2002, put on by Oakland's Lake Merritt United Methodist Church. Calls went out to locate over a hundred pieces. Madeline just went along, very proud, but not thinking she had done anything special.

Monique Beeler of ANG Newspapers saw the show May 6, 2002 – a celebration for Madeline's 100th – and described the dolls in this way: "A few of them are boy dolls dressed in striped and colorful polo shirts, but the majority of long, leggy dolls wear flouncy, lace-trimmed dresses in pale pink, butter yellow or sailor-suit blue. Their thick black yarn hair pokes out from their heads in a cheerful tangle and all wear smiles, often with white embroidered teeth showing." Beaming, Madeline recalls that display of her work.

"Do what you're able to do and make use of what you have."

Madeline owns her house in Oakland, as she will tell you a hundred times and still want to tell you again. It's been paid off for years, a fact she's very proud of, for the house is the symbol of her independence. The man next door still comes around every so often and wants to buy it. "Where will I live?" Madeline asks. "At my place next door. I have rooms upstairs," he says. "Oh no," she replies. "I don't want you to raise the rent or get me thrown out in the street." She likes her own wood-framed green house because it's small, just big enough for one or two people with no space for roomers, whom you never can trust.

She tells me her story. She was born and raised in Philadelphia where she spent the greater part of her life before coming to California. Her mother, a single parent for most of Madeline's childhood, had already raised another daughter, fifteen years older. Madeline was about twenty before she met her sister who, sadly, died shortly afterwards.

She knows nothing about her father because Madeline's mother refused to discuss him. "I used to go to Sunday school and church on Sundays, and one Sunday I decided to find out. I would seek out men who were as black as me, 'Are you my father? Are you my father?' I would ask."

Madeline was a boarder more often than she cares to remember. Her mother cooked for various hotels and restaurants, and in the summers Madeline accompanied her when she went to cook at hotels in and around Atlantic City. While working, she would leave Madeline at a boardinghouse where, surprisingly considering her ebullient nature, Madeline says, "I never felt wanted."

She recalls one place where everyone adored a boy her age and told

Madeline with plaster piece, Laney Art Show, age 68

him, "You'll really go somewhere one day." But Madeline got no praise, and in fact felt ignored. "You're never gonna get anywhere," they told her, and she thinks she knows why. "He had good hair. I had bad hair. It was because I was so black, and he was cookie-colored brown."

Her mother features grandly in her memories. "She encouraged me to go to school and get an education." Things she said are important still to Madeline, things like, "You be who you are, not what somebody else wants you to be," and, "They all stuck up, we're not like them," referring to some black neighbors. Her mother taught her to count on herself alone, and to learn to support herself and be independent. "Do what you're able to do and make use of what you have."

Thanks to her mother, she developed enormous self-respect and the determination to fend for herself. After high school, she applied to a nursing school for black women only. The administration was impressed with her application and telephone interview, and invited her to a personal interview. But when she went, Madeline was politely told that she was not accepted. She assumes that she failed "the paper bag test: if you were darker than a paper bag, you were too black."

Pillows 1993-1997: "'As I go along the ideas come and I try to carry them out.' She used the wrong side of the fabric for one of her pillows because it was 'more alive,' and stuck a small patch in the corner of a second to 'say hello to the other patches.'" Courtesy of Eli Leon, Oakland, CA

Fortunately, "I was admitted to the Lincoln School of Nursing in New York, started by a wealthy Caucasian woman who wanted black women to be nurses." Madeline paid the $25 fee and set off for New York with suitcase in hand. In 1926 she was one of 25 graduates, and became one of the few black nurses in the country.

She has fond memories of her nursing school days; she loved learning and made several good friends. She is grateful to her patron, the "wealthy Caucasian woman," for making her career possible. "I liked to take care of the patients – like all people – some are nice, some aren't so nice. If people aren't so nice I just tolerate them. I did the best I could with them."

For most of her career she worked in the medical unit of the U.S. Post Office. Madeline also had stints in the Public Health Service in New York, where she worked in schools, at a well-baby clinic, in a psychiatric unit, and served as a home health nurse going house to house.

Although she married, her husband died of tuberculosis around 1933 when their daughter was just an infant. She and Clara lived mostly in New York, first Staten Island, then the Bronx. Two of her nursing school colleagues stayed at their home at various times and helped Madeline raise Clara.

Madeline in Alaska, middle of photo, 1980

This was in the 1930s and she felt fortunate to have a job. Madeline remembers many people begging on the streets. Then came World War II and food rationing, but somehow she always managed. She recalls, "There wasn't much meat." She had chances to remarry but chose not to because "I couldn't count on them treating my child the way I wanted to treat her. You know, they always think of them as the stepchild. So I decided to raise her myself."

After she retired and moved to the Bay Area, she put her bustling energy not only into her art, but into volunteer work for 25 years – at a hospital, of course. Highland Hospital was the lucky recipient of her labors, this time not as a nurse but in the office where her warmth and caring raised everyone's spirits. "What I believe is," says Madeline, "treat people as you would *like* to be treated, not as people treat you."

In 2003, Feather River Camp in the California foothills was in a struggle with the City of Oakland. The funding the city needed to maintain the camp was on the line. Madeline, still peppy at 101, and an avid camper (yes, tent camping with restrooms down the road), was asked to speak before the City Council about the importance of maintaining the camp.

Her persuasions won over the City Council and it found the funding for the camp.

In August, 2005 the 103 year old Madeline and her daughter Clara Sims set off on a trip to Alaska! In past years Madeline traveled with her daughter and granddaughter to China and Africa. "I have a picture of her on a camel," Clara says. "She still loves the memories of those trips immensely, especially the reverence so many people showed her as an elder."

These days, Madeline seems happy with her routine of going to the senior center twice a week for socializing and seeing her daughter and grandchildren when she can. "I pray before I go to bed every night for God to help me and to help somebody else. I end by saying The Lord's Prayer. Then I go to sleep peacefully. As for trying to get revenge on people – just because someone does something to you, doesn't mean you have to do it back... I've had a good life, I can't complain."

Asked what makes getting up in the morning worthwhile, she answers, "The morning's a new day, so you wake up, you might as well get up. You have things to do. You're living, God gave you life, you have a right to live, so you might as well find something interesting to do. Sooner or later you can help someone along the way."

Postscript: *Madeline is an artist who has let the* sturm and drang *of former years drift away. She does not remember the anxieties, or tension over the many decisions she made in order to create all she did. It seems to her at this age, "I just did it." My belief is that a peaceful inner self is most important to her at this point in her life, and she has achieved it. She has found a mechanism to sift out not only the details, but the strains and stresses of her artistic life. She remembers it now as an easy ebb and flow.*

Madeline at 101 with her creations

Isabel at 89. "Get Your Vegetables Here"   Photo: Phillip Kaake

Of creativity: "An unexpected flash of a different recognition." And, "A non-acceptance of the given." Then, "An unfamiliar look at the familiar."

Reflections More Light than Dark
ISABEL FERGUSON
aka BETTY PETERSON
ACTOR, ILLUSTRATOR, PAINTER, ASSEMBLAGE ARTIST
Born November 9, 1916

"I see… That's what artists do. They look, they see.
I see things that I can sometimes put together. It's a discovery."

Isabel's art runs wild – collages, paintings, fanciful sculptures of found objects – a typewriter in its case, emblazoned with "The Great American Novel," a red toy car parked in front of a skyscraper built of old slide holders with a satellite dish way up top, and the title, "Honey I'm Home." Among my favorites: a set of four Campbell soup cans, their labels replaced by Andy Warhol images.

I was immediately struck by her impishly styled light brown reddish hair, pixie smile and shining eyes. Nearly 90, she seems more a fey young woman about to fly.

Isabel's light, airy one-bedroom apartment in Oakland, California is like an art gallery. Beautifully arranged paintings hang on all walls, assemblages are strikingly placed throughout. In the small kitchen displayed around her 1940s toaster are original drawings, such as "the bicyclettist," with a photo of Isabel poking through one of the wheels, wooden plaques with found sayings like, "A GROWING MUSHROOM can push its way through three inches of asphalt," for example. All the art is her own.

Isabel's bedroom artfully doubles as a sitting room. The closet, a sort of prop room, is filled with sculptures and curious creations. Styrofoam heads with curlers and green eyelashes and Polaroids mounted on various wood

Isabel and mother, 1917

frames fill the small space. "They have a presence," Isabel says.

On an end table is a tall candle surrounded by spent matches – an assemblage called "The Virgin." They just didn't get to her, so the candle remains unlit.

"I collect strange items and people know that and give me things…" Isabel continues speaking in her run-on way, hardly pausing to take a breath. "A friend brought me a wonderful looking key. It was large and quite heavy. It looked like a key to a dungeon. I thought that would make a perfect light cord pull. I climbed up on a chair to affix it. The chair slid out from under me. Down I came, hard, and that's how an artist breaks a hip!"

She was then 84. Recovering from her hip operation and dependent on a cane, she nonetheless felt compelled to fulfill additional artistic dreams. She wanted to write plays and act. So she sought out Stagebridge in Oakland, California – the oldest theater for seniors in the country, ongoing since 1978.

"I joined Stagebridge because a class in play writing was being offered. I'd always wanted to write, but the class lacked attendance. So I joined the improv and acting classes and it has been quite wonderful."

Long interested in acting, she was eager to do something about her voice. "It seemed to me so *feeble*! Linda (Spector) helped me find my new voice. She is such a good teacher, so patient, so affirmative. You cannot make a mistake, you cannot do anything wrong. She just told us it comes from here," patting her diaphragm. "I really think it's a matter of confidence." Whatever the art is of instilling confidence in someone, Stagebridge offers it.

I had read about her role in *Being Something*, a humorous, touching play exploring intergenerational as well as inter-racial themes directed by Ellen Sebastian Chang, and performed in spring 2005. This was Isabel's fifth year at Stagebridge. "I loved doing that play, especially because it meant so much to my great-grandson. He's 16 and was so proud of me." Isabel has two grandchildren and two great-grands.

"When I joined Stagebridge, I decided to use my middle name, Isabel, rather than Betty which I had been called all my life. It suits me so much better."

Isabel was born in London during a World War I air raid. "There were zeppelins flying overhead... and most of the family ran to the basement... but my mother couldn't get there, and she went under the dining room table. At least that's the story," she says. "My father was Canadian, in France, flying with the RAF. He never got over the war. And then there was another baby." When Isabel was three, the family moved to British Columbia because Canada gave you land if you were willing to homestead it.

"My father could never be inside again after the war. For my mother it must have been awful, a rich English girl who had been to art school, and now in British Columbia with nothing. She had to learn to do everything. As they say, she didn't know how to boil an egg. She didn't have to. We tried chickens. We had a cow. We lived off vegetables and eggs, and my mother learned to bake bread, make butter..."

They turned out not to be very good farmers. "It was a miserable marriage, but they tried everything. Then my father left. I was little. And then he came back. And then he left for good."

It was a difficult childhood, but "I'm a survivor," remarks Isabel. Her mother remarried a British colonel and stayed in British Columbia. Her stepfather wasn't trained to make a living "but the best shot in the countryside – we ate a great deal of pheasant and duck and grouse. I remember biting down on the shot." She whines in the small voice with the English accent she had as a child,

Dancing days, 1940

New Year's Eve, 1941, Isabel in stripes

"Oh mommy, can't we please have some hamburger?"

After boarding school in Vancouver, a strict and cold one, Isabel was sent to New York. "That was very difficult. My father, in New York by now and remarried, had a wife six feet tall and part Cherokee. She'd been a reporter for the old *New York World* and a graduate from the first class of Wellesley. Then, amazingly for a woman in the early 1930s, she opened two restaurants.

She was trés formidable.

"She didn't know what to do with me. They sent me to business school which was a disaster. I'm not that type [pun?], so I went to the Art Students League."

Despite the Depression, New York was wonderful in the 1930s. "Jazz!! All up and down 52nd Street. And Big Band dancing! Went out dancing every night, to the Rainbow Room or whatever it was called. And I did the absolutely classic thing of running after the milk wagon at dawn to get milk bottles – they had milk bottles in those days."

Isabel went to art classes during the day, then had to work in one of her stepmother's midtown restaurants, The Cherry Tree or The Lion and the Lamb, before she could go out dancing.

She met her husband, a roommate of a fellow art student, and lived some time in Brooklyn Heights, managing on very little money. "We were struggling to put food on the table. My husband worked in advertising at Abraham and Strauss." A daughter, Penelope, was born in 1939.

They moved to Boston when her husband started working at Filenes department store, and living in Cambridge, Isabel took writing classes at Adult Extension at Harvard. "We moved out here in 1949, where my husband got a job."

Always Isabel did some form of volunteer work. "When my daughter was little I used to read to a blind man." Later she volunteered with the Oakland Library's project in literacy, Second Start, and worked with many adults teaching them to read for the first time. "I care so much about language. And I feel strange if I don't volunteer." Her daughter Penelope has volunteered at the Alta Bates Summit Medical Center in Berkeley for twenty-one years. Isabel and Penelope decided that "it was in the genes to volunteer."

In the 1950s Isabel's marriage fell apart. "I took a Berkeley Extension class so I could get back into my art. After the divorce, I had to make some money." Moving to San Francisco she did children's portraits, which proved difficult. "People don't see their children the way I saw them. I went up to Parnassus Press to see if I could do some cut and paste. But talk about serendipity! They gave me a children's book to do." There was no juvenile press around and Parnassus wanted non-commercial artists to do their children's books.

Isabel illustrated three children's books under the name Betty Peterson. "By that time [late1950s], I was divorced but kept my married name to please my mother-in-law."

Her first assignment was *The Bunny Who Found Easter,* published by Parnassus Press in 1959. "My idea was to use brush and water color, and I went to Tilden Park every day to sketch bunnies." The book, by Charlotte Zolotow, now

Isabel and daughter Penelope, Cambridge, Mass, 1943
Photo: John Vincent

a famous children's author, received considerable press attention. "Betty Peterson's charming, simple water-color pictures, soft, wavy, black outlines with splashes of very clear, luminous blues, greens and yellows, has caught a feeling for Easter that surely will appeal to the very young and to those who read aloud to them," *The Herald Tribune Book Review*, March, 1959. The book enjoyed great success and Isabel received royalties for years.

She also illustrated *Best of Friends* by Josephine Haskell Aldredge, Parnassus Press, Berkeley, California, 1963. *Bravo Marco* was the next. For this charming tale, printed in English with an Italian translation, Isabel says she spent weeks researching the customs and culture of Sicily.

"And then I didn't do any more of that. I just stopped illustrating books. I started doing more three dimensional things. I painted, studying with Norman Stiegmuller at adult education classes in San Francisco." Betty (Isabel) had her own show at the Unicorn Gallery, long gone, on Fillmore Street in San Francisco, and she was part of several group shows. "I decided on cages for one of them – bird cages. I did all kinds of cages. That seemed to be my thing, this three-dimensional stuff."

"Betty Ferguson [she had reverted to her maiden name] manages to combine the best tradition of Dada incongruity with Zen surprise," wrote Tom Albright, *San Francisco Chronicle*, 1966. Isabel showed her work every few years at various galleries in the Bay Area. Her last solo show was in 1995 at the Vesuvio Café, North Beach, San Francisco; her last group show, in 1996, was at the Center for Visual Arts, Oakland.

Isabel moved from San Francisco to the East Bay around 1980 and managed to keep financially afloat with clerical jobs and cat-sitting. After her ex-husband Henry Peterson died, she received his social security. She was able to move to an interesting apartment building on Park Boulevard in Oakland, nicknamed Le Château for its faux French façade. She lived there 15 years.

"Old age is hot right now. They don't know what to do with us!"

"Then I fell. My daughter, always loving, ever helpful, in fact, was invaluable. She moved me while I was in a rest home and I never got back to Le Château. There was no elevator and it was a 72 steps-up-from-the-street-apartment (the grandchildren counted them). I recuperated for six weeks after breaking my hip. You have to learn to walk again. It's a lot of work. A lot of people give up because it's so much work."

But Isabel is more interested in the present than the past. She wants to talk about Stagebridge. "Last year they hired an artist in residence – Henk Smits, a wonderful Dutch dancer and choreographer, 6'4" "who can curl up like a pretzel or be airborne… He was going to do something interesting with dance and movement.

"He uses props. Those orange traffic cones. He hadn't been in California before but he thought everyone was afraid," she says. "It was called 'The Danger Project.'"

Henk gave them paper and pencil and asked, "What are you afraid of? How are you afraid?" Isabel continued,

Isabel with art, 1960

"I wrote down things I was told to be afraid of. I remember my only sexual education when my mother said, 'careful Betty, it can happen in a car!' and that became part of the performance.

"One person said, 'I'm afraid of fire' – so that became part of the performance. And, what else, crossing the street. Each fear became a dance. I said, 'Yes, it can happen in a car.' And then there was a pause, and I said, 'and it did!'" And there were gales of laughter.

"We worked and worked and then we opened in Las Vegas! There was a national senior theater project and a wonderful theater there, and we were invited to open in Vegas. That was the first time I'd ever been on stage!"

Soon they were doing another piece. "I said to Henk, 'I'm sick, I'm moving, the apartment is filled with boxes and boxes.' And that became part of the next performance. Instead of cones, there were boxes. And it was about me. It was about an old woman moving – as she looks at the boxes they seem to her to be full of memories." The memories were also drawn from Isabel's real life, about her first love (a platonic one) with Doug at 14.

1981, Morning - early! Isabel in Toronto, in a multi-media show, Phantom Oasis. Photo: Dennis Hunkler

In her seventies, Isabel realized her lifelong dream of visiting Paris. Her first day there she rushed to the bookstore Shakespeare and Company and marveled, "Books, books, books… And I was invited to tea on the second floor!" She enrolled in a painting class where most of the students were young and had little English. Her French was "mauvais," she laments, but their common language was art. She lived Paris to the hilt, even rented the tiny attic room of her dreams. "It was just heaven. I'm very emotional about Paris.

"Every day it seemed there were adventures, large or small. One day I'm sure I found the apartment where Colette lived in the Palais Royale."

These days, she's excited about her theater work and her volunteer job as drama assistant at Piedmont Gardens, a senior residence. "Last year I wrote a one-act, but it was too difficult to put on. There were so many health problems and a lot of memory loss. We were working with assisted living residents, people in wheelchairs. What we're doing now is improv, which works much better."

When one of the women in the class improvised with a paper plate, she held it up as a mirror and said, "Oh, how I've aged." Isabel was delighted that she'd excited her imagination.

When asked about creativity, Isabel defines it variously. "An unexpected flash of a different recognition." And, "A non-acceptance of the given." Then, "An unfamiliar look at the familiar."

At the Stagebridge library, students seek out monologues to memorize. "We put all the monologues together and made one into a play – called it *Reunion*." They took it to three senior homes this year. "I wrote my monologue, instead of using a prepared one.

"*Luna,* it's called. I feel strongly about it. I want us to leave the moon alone. That's the idea of it. Afterwards I was told one woman had tears in her eyes. I was very happy about that. It means my monologue worked."

*"I Didn't See or Hear a Thing,"
1990*

Were you in costume? I ask. "Yes. I looked disheveled. In my piece I had apparently escaped from a retirement home, seemed a little deranged. No, I've never been in a rest home, or a sanitarium. They'll never get me into one." She takes a deep breath.

The Apple, *Isabel on left, 2004*

"We did a piece (in *Being Something*) about an old woman who would not go to a rest home. She made a pest of herself. Her brother decided if workers were checking on her that it would be okay. She fought very hard to stay at home."

She adds, "Old age is hot right now. They don't know what to do with us!"

Isabel pauses. We share some ripe figs and cream cheese. "Art is what interests me." She continues, thinking of food and art. "I'm the one who organizes picnics with my fine, talented friends. Two years ago I organized one à la Manet's "*Dejeuner Sur L'Herbe*," in the Redwoods. We made a tableau as in the painting. Over lunch we wrote stream of consciousness poetry. My idea was that the women wear clothes and the men not. The men decided we were just too close to the public road – but they did take their shirts off."

By now I know I'm in the presence of an artist, and a dramatic one. "You put a canvas on a table," Isabel says. "If you're going to do something, you don't need a studio. I did these paintings summer before last in my old place, a one room apartment." She points towards dozens of canvases standing up against and lining the living room walls.

She selects her latest painting, of chanterelles. "After seeing these yesterday, the golden color, I just had to paint them. I couldn't not.

"Paul Klee says it very well for me." In translation, "I create so I won't cry."

She has stacks of small books she calls *Flowers* and *Fish,* recently made. Each page has a new thought with one of her drawings reduced. Some of them read: "The sky looked strange but reliable;" and, "They were all tired of subterfuge; Once it was decided, they hurried away; The sky looked calm but alert; No beaver's without a dam, he cried, feeling silly." The text on the page has nothing to do with the art work – "It's DADA here," remarks Isabel.

No surprise, Isabel writes stories and poetry. Here are recent ones:

Have You Noticed

Have you noticed

That the teacups are half full of sand?

That the piano, moving fast, just passed us on the right?

And that the clouds are full of birds afraid to fly?

Mortality

Perhaps leave

A trace – or two –

On that sweet blank sand?

No –

The tide comes in

Quite fast, really –

Footprints fill

Vanish,

End.   May, 2006

At the end of the day, Isabel is thinking, "It's 5 o'clock – do you know where my martini is?"

And when does she do her art? "Whenever the muse flies in. Sometimes she doesn't stay. 'The muse flew in and flew right out, forgot my song I have no doubt.'"

A very short, short story, 2005   *Photo: Phillip Kaake*

AMY GORMAN
AUTHOR

Aging Artfully is the synthesis of Amy Gorman's experience working with aging and in the arts. Her work as a young speech therapist at V.A. Hospitals and later as a medical social worker with dementia and Alzheimer's patients led to her service as a board member at Lifelong Medical Care/ Over 60 Clinic in Oakland, California, which addresses the medical and social needs of the aged.

Amy founded Kidshows in 1982, a non-profit arts organization, to introduce children to the arts, live theater, music, dance and storytelling. During her 18 years as its Executive Director, the professional performers she worked with shared many concerns about getting older, and whether or not they could continue earning a living in their chosen art form.

She lives with her husband, George, in Berkeley – says she married him because of his resonant voice, also because he keeps her laughing. Their two adult sons, Ari and Phil, both professional musicians, live in the Bay Area.

Besides hanging out with women artists over 85, and shmoozing with many friends, she likes to sculpt ceramic heads, scuba dive in the tropics, hike in the desert, and watch penguins.

FRANCES KANDL
COMPOSER

Frances Kandl, who wrote songs about some of the women portrayed in Aging Artfully, has been writing music since the age of five. Her first composition, "The Tiger Cat," consisted of a series of c-major chords, culminating in several dissonant grace-notes and a crashing tone cluster (full forearm percussion) representing the cat scampering over a table and toppling a vase. She has since attempted to develop a greater degree of subtlety in her composition. Fortunately none of the women in these songs was inclined to climb on tables or break crockery. Ms. Kandl lives in Berkeley in a house with Nico, Mari, and Peter, who embody all the reasons she wouldn't live anywhere else. She loves vibrant old women and aspires to be one.